© Danann Publishing Limited 2024

First published in the UK by Sona Books, an imprint of Danann Publishing Limited

WARNING: For private domestic use only, any unauthorised copying, hiring, lending or public performance of this book is illegal.

CAT NO. SONO556

Photography courtesy of Getty Images

CBS Photo Archive	Jamie Mccarthy	Kirstin Sinclair	Roger Kisby
Christopher Polk	Ollie Millington	Dave Benett	Mondadori Portfolio
John Keeble	Blue Sky In My Pocket	Tim P. Whitby	Francesco Prandoni
Armend Nimani	David M. Benett	Dave J Hogan	

Photography courtesy of Alamy Stock Photo

Edward.J.Westmacott	ZUMA Press, Inc.	Jordan Strauss/Invision/AP	Katy Blackwood
Mairo Cinquetti	Everett Collection Inc	Rob Grabowski/AP	DPA Picture Alliance
Doug Peters	Gregg Deguire/UPI	Evan Agostini/AP	Image Press Agency
Michele Ursi	Mickael Chavet / Project	Luca Bruno/AP	Landmark Media
WENN Rights Ltd	Daybreak	Visar Kryeziu/AP	Nils Jorgensen
Will Bailey	Chris Pizzello/AP	Barry King	

Other images, Wiki Commons

Cover design: Darren Grice
Book design: Kate Cerpnjak
Editor: Sofia Della Valle
Proof reader: Juliette O'Neill
Cover image: Dan MacMedan

All rights reserved. No Part of this title may be reproduced or transmitted in any material form (including photocopying or storing it in any medium by electronic means and whether or not transiently or incidentally to some other use of this publication) without the written permission of the copyright owner, except in accordance with the provisions of the Copyright, Designs and Patents Act 1988. Applications for the copyright owner's written permission should be addressed to the publisher.

This is an independent publication and it is unofficial and unauthorised and as such has no connection with the artist or artists featured, their management or any other organisation connected in any way whatsoever with the artist or artists featured in the book.

Printed in EU

ISBN: 978-1-915343-74-1

Dua Lipa

MWAH

Carolyn McHugh

Dua Lipa MWAH

Wireless Festival, London 2016.

Contents

Introduction 8
Dreams (1995-2010) 10
Breaking through (2010-2015) 18
The early singles (2015-2017) 22
Dua's dazzling debut album (2017) 36
Superstardom (2018-2019) 46
Future Nostalgia (2020) 60
Smash Hit Singles 70
Owning lockdown 74
The tours 80
Skilful songwriting 98
Queen of collaborations 104
A passion for fashion 114
Making a difference 122
Radical optimism for Dua's continued success..... 128
Discography 138
Go Dua! 140

Dua Lipa MWAH

Introduction

From viral sensation to Grammy award-winning global superstar, Dua Lipa is currently the most streamed UK artist in the world. In just a few years, the British/Kosovan singer-songwriter has established herself as the doyenne of 'dark pop' with a succession of upbeat catchy hit tracks with dark lyrics and undertones.

She's also the queen of collaboration, sought after for her vocals and creative input by the industry's leading and most dynamic artists, producers and DJs including Calvin Harris, Mark Ronson and Diplo as well as long-established legends of earlier eras such as Chris Martin and Elton John.

Born and raised in London to Kosovan/Albanian parents, Dua Lipa signed to Warner Records in 2014 and released her self-titled debut album two years later, featuring the hit singles 'Be the One', 'IDGAF', 'Hotter Than Hell' and her first UK #1 single 'New Rules'. Her acclaimed follow up album, Future Nostalgia, consolidated her alpha female status as she continued to provide the soundtrack to the lives of young women the world over with more hit songs, including One Kiss, Levitating, Physical and Don't Start Now. Her highly anticipated third album, Radical Optimism, went straight to the top of the charts in May 2024 including chart-topping tracks Houdini and Training Season.

With her albums selling in their multi-millions, her stadium tours all sell-outs, and three Grammys and seven Brit Awards to her name, Dua is one of the hardest working women in music. She has a strong sense of the visual which means her live shows are must-sees - she owns the stage and goes all out to give high energy performances incorporating pin-sharp choreography and stunning costume changes. Fans liken her to a goddess, with one describing her as a 'super model who can sing'.

Her powerful and distinctive voice has been compared to Joss Stone and Lady Gaga, while Rolling Stone magazine describes her as '...a cross between Amy Winehouse and Nelly Furtado'.

Every song is a bop and, with her signature disco/pop and R&B sound, Dua Lipa kickstarted this decade's trend of bringing an updated 1980s sound to a new generation. She's the real deal - a legitimate pop sensation - and this is her story so far ......

Introduction

Dua Lipa performs on The Pyramid stage at Glastonbury, 2024.

Dua Lipa MWAH

Dreams (1995-2010)

When Dua Lipa first broke through in the UK with her 2016 hit Hotter Than Hell she seemed almost to have sprung out of nowhere. Was she a manufactured pop star? A beautiful girl picked by a label for her looks and malleability. Even her name sounded made up. Yet nothing could be further from the truth. Dua Lipa is her real name – 'Dua' means love in her native Albania - and she had put

DETAILS ON DUA

BIRTHDAY: Born in London on 22 August 1995

HEIGHT: 5 ft 8ins (1.73m)

EYES: Light brown

EARLY MUSICAL INFLUENCES: Nelly Furtado and Pink.

FIRST ALBUM SHE BOUGHT: Whoa, Nelly! by Nelly Furtado

RIGHT: Dua on stage at Capital's Jingle Bell Ball at the O2 Arena in London, 2016.

Dreams (1995-2010)

in years of groundwork as she dedicated herself to her career in music.

Dua had always had big dreams. She started singing when she was five years old and by the time she was a teenager, she was determined to write and perform her own music. Dua was born on 22 August 1995 and grew up in North London, after her Albanian parents, Dukagjin and Anesa Lipa, left their native Kosovo in 1992 and came to live in the UK to escape the unrest and problems of their homeland at that time. She has two younger siblings, a sister Rina and brother Gjin.

BELOW: Dua's parents at the Brit Awards 2019.

Kosovo is a small country in the Balkans which declared independence from Serbia in 2008. Both Kosovo and Serbia were formerly part of the state of Yugoslavia where there had long been tensions between Kosovo's Albanian and Serb communities, culminating in major violence and, eventually, the 1998/99 Kosovo War.

Dua Lipa MWAH

FUN FACT
Following Dua's rise to fame with New Rules, the number of babies named Dua in the UK doubled, growing from 63 in 2017 to 126 in 2019.

Back home in Kosovo her parents had been at university and her father Dukagjin had also been lead singer of the Kosovan rock band Oda. But in London he and his wife, like many refugees, had to start over and take whatever employment they could find, which included working in hospitality and marketing.

Through it all, Dukagjin's love of music remained and his career as a musician was a major influence on young Dua who was exposed to all kinds of different music at home, including David Bowie, Bob Dylan, the Stereophonics and Radiohead. As she got older she became a big fan of Nelly Furtado and Pink and

NELLY FURTADO

BOB DYLAN

PINK

Dreams (1995-2010)

credits the mix of rock, pop and hip-hop styles with shaping her own voice. Not that her vocal abilities were appreciated by everyone in the early days - when she auditioned to join the school choir aged 11, she couldn't make the high notes and a teacher told her she couldn't sing.

But she was otherwise happily settled in London, where she attended Parliament Hill, a state comprehensive school, next to Hampstead Heath, which more than holds its own among the private schools that surround it. She also attended the acclaimed Sylvia Young Theatre School on Saturdays for training in singing, drama, and dance.

Life was good. But then, midway through senior school, Dua's life was turned upside down when her parents decided to move back to Kosovo after the country declared independence in February 2008 and the situation there had settled down. Dua was 13, a tricky time for any young girl to leave her London life and friendships behind and start over in what was, for her, a foreign country. However she was determined to make the best of it, having always been proud of her Albanian heritage.

ABOVE: Parliament Hill and Sylvia Young Theatre School, North London.

Dua Lipa MWAH

Her family had always spoken both English and Albanian at home so at least there was no language barrier. Nevertheless Dua has spoken of initially struggling to fit in, but eventually she settled down and she made friends at her new Mileniumi i Tretë School.

It was around this time, while living back in Kosovo, that her determination to work in the music business really crystalised. American hip hop was massive in Kosovo and Dua grew to love it. The first concert she ever went to was American hip hop duo Method Man & Redman and the second was another American rapper, 50 Cent.

By the time she was 15, Dua knew that she wanted to make a career in music. But this was never going to be easy while she was living in Kosovo, where she couldn't see the same opportunities for a musical career as there would be in London. So, inspired by the impact and success of Canadian singer Justin Bieber had enjoyed by breaking through on social media, she decided to share

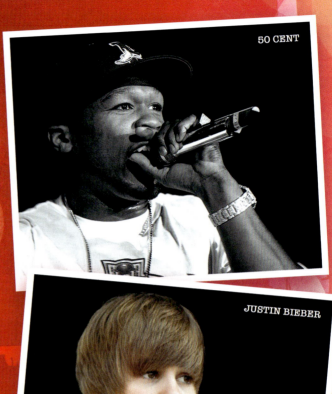

50 CENT

JUSTIN BIEBER

'I wanted people around me to know what I do, and it felt like the easiest way for me to be able to just get my stuff out - I didn't really know how else I was going to have people hear me'.

Dreams (1995-2010)

her voice in similar fashion by covering songs by her favourite singers and posting them on YouTube. 'I just wanted my friends in school to know I was singing,' Dua said in a later interview with YouTube.

She knew she had to get back to the UK to take music classes and make the most of the greater openings there. After months of making her case, she eventually persuaded her parents to let her move back to London without them and follow her dream of becoming a pop star.

Speaking about how grateful she is to her parents for allowing her to return to the UK she said, 'I couldn't do music the way that I wanted to in Kosovo. Maybe things would've been different if streaming services were as prominent as they are now but, for me, London was always home, and I found my footing very quickly.'

It was arranged that Dua would travel back to North London and live with some old family friends in Camden. She arrived back in the UK in 2010 and worked hard to pay her way while she focussed on her music and figured out how to break through. Talking to NME about the transition of living alone at such a young age Dua said; 'The realisation that no one was going to clear up after me was tough! But stuff like that really made me grow up before my time. It helped me mature I guess and made me who I am today. I'm really grateful for it, but I do remember it being a struggle.'

Dua finished school and took a gap year to focus on her career. During this time she did various part time jobs including working as a nightclub hostess. The saying goes that no experience is wasted, and certainly this slice of London's slightly darker nightlife inspired many of her song themes and lyrics – as she puts it herself; 'The dramas every night, the dark side of nightlife, they became something I wanted to write about'.

Little did she know that these early life experiences would become so useful in the sensational career she was about to embark upon.

Camden Town, North London.

Dua Lipa MWAH

Dua attends the Mount Street Christmas Lights switch on featuring the launch of Julian The Bear, in aid of Great Ormond Street Hospital Children's Charity, 2015.

Dua Lipa MWAH

Breaking Through (2010-2015)

Settled back in London, Dua continued to use social media to her advantage by uploading her covers to YouTube. Her repertoire had expanded to include acts like Jessie J and Joss Stone and, although she was singing other people's songs, Dua was beginning to find her own sound. Her collection of covers was becoming a giant show reel of her work. Her voice was out there and whenever she did meet anyone connected with the music business she would get them to check out her channel, chancing her luck by suggesting;

> 'If you like them and my voice maybe we should work together'.

One of the ways she began to make connections was through modelling. She wasn't especially interested in making a career out of being a model but was smart enough to realise the crossover between various branches of the entertainment industry. So when she was scouted by the leading fashion management agency Next Management, which specialises in connecting top talent in fashion and entertainment, she took on some assignments in the hope of making contacts in the music industry.

JOSS STONE

It was while she was modelling that she appeared in an advertisement for the UK's The X Factor talent show, leading to later speculation that she had been a contestant. But she did not appear on the actual show, just in an advertisement for it, when she sang Lost in Music.

JESSIE J

Breaking through (2010-2015)

LEFT: Dua Lipa on day 2 of London Collections: Men on June 17, 2013 in London, England.

BELOW: Dua Lipa on day 2 of London Fashion Week Spring/Summer 2013, at Somerset House on September 14, 2013 in London, England.

Meanwhile, she took every opportunity to promote her YouTube channel and began uploading her first original songs to SoundCloud in 2012. By the time she was 18, her YouTube covers, including Alicia Key's If I Ain't Got You and Christina Aguilera's Beautiful, were gaining attention. 'It created a portfolio for me and then I started getting messages from producers and people saying like "Hey if you want to come and use the studio you can come and just write" and that's how it started', said Dua.

Dua Lipa MWAH

All her hard work and tenacity paid off when her channel was viewed by top music manager Ben Mawson who, with his partner Ed Millett, ran leading management company TaP Music which was already looking after Lana Del Rey. Reflecting on his first meeting with Dua, Ben Mawson said:

'She came into our office and the first thing that struck me was just how incredibly charismatic she was. She had bags of ambition and she played us little bits of demos and the voice was just amazing'.

TaP Music wasted no time in signing Dua and, under this new management team, Dua went on to sign a record deal with Warner Records in 2014. Ever savvy, she didn't give up her day job at a restaurant until the ink was dry on the deal.

As Ed Millett recalls, 'Dua was really smart – she signed to Warner Bros. partly because they didn't have a big female pop artist and they needed one. They really wanted her, so she had the focus of the team from day one'.

With the might of Warner behind her, all sorts of doors began to open and soon, Dua got the chance to work with hugely successful American music producer Emile Haynie, producer of artists including Eminem and Bruno Mars, as well as Lana Del Rey.

She spent a couple of years working on material and putting out singles, seeing what would stick.

The result was Dua's first single New Love, released in August 2015. A few months later, her second single, Be the One, gave her the breakthrough she needed, although it was a slow burner.

Both these early releases helped get Dua noticed. Then she received a massive boost when she was featured by the BBC in its Sound of 2016 list which showcased the UK's most exciting and innovative rising stars.

Breaking through (2010-2015)

With great prescience, the list's organisers described Dua as looking and sounding like a pop star in waiting, saying she was 'smoky of voice and sultry of photo' with 'an off-kilter, it-girl sound, powered by [her] deep resonant voice; one that's a world away from the thinly auto-tuned sound of most radio-bound pop'.

In January 2016, she began her first tour through the UK and Europe, which continued till November. That same year she also did some gigs supporting Australian YouTube sensation Troye Sivan.

Crowds were receptive. Momentum was building.

Dua was on her way.

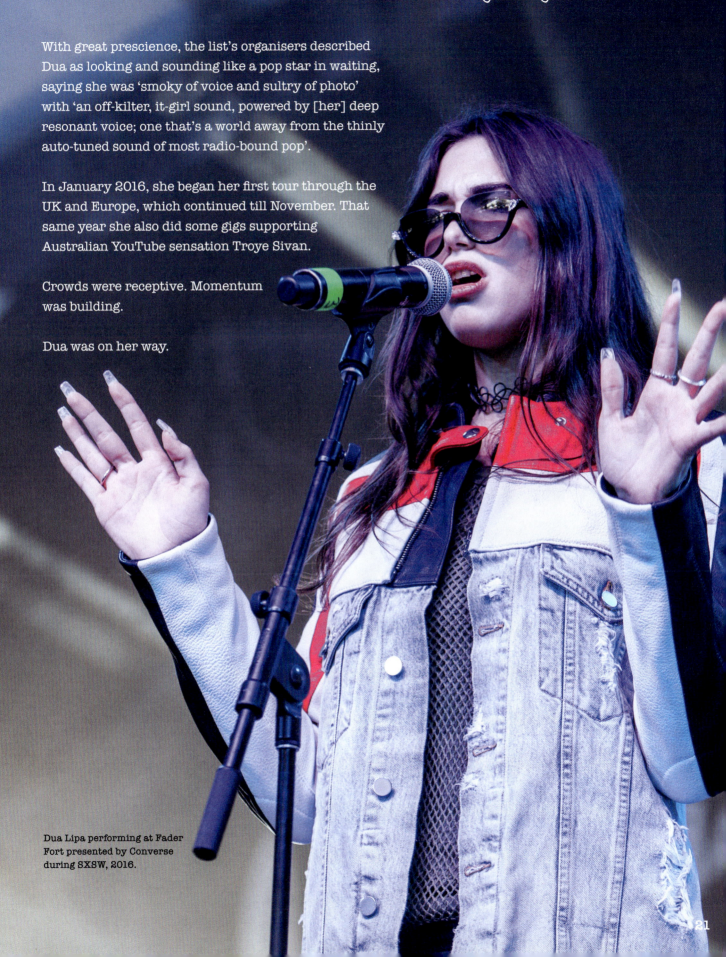

Dua Lipa performing at Fader Fort presented by Converse during SXSW, 2016.

Dua Lipa MWAH!

The early singles (2015-2017)

New Love - August 2015
New Love was Dua's debut single, which she wrote herself with producers Emile Haynie and Andrew Wyatt, and it was about her struggle for success in the music business. While it sounds like a love song it's in fact about Dua trying to find her place in the industry and facing the fear of losing 'the only thing that matters to you'. Critics liked it, praising her vocals, variously described as 'beautiful' and sounding 'older than her years', but the track didn't make an impact on the charts.

Be the One - October 2015
Written by Dua's friend Lucy Taylor, alongside Digital Farm Animals and Jack Tarrant, Be the One was about miscommunication in a relationship. Although Dua loved the song, she was initially reluctant to record someone else's composition as she generally prefers to have experienced the lyrics she sings. However she gave it a try, found it fun to perform and made it her own.

The track when down well with music critics who particularly praised Dua's smoky, rich, and lush vocals. It received little recognition and not much airplay at first, but was a sleeper hit, gradually creeping up the charts, first in Germany, then in Austria, Hungary, Slovenia and Poland, before peaking in the Netherlands where it reached #11 in the charts and achieved double platinum sales. By April 2016 the track was a hit in Australia and New Zealand. It eventually made the UK charts in January 2017 where it entered at #70, rising to a peak of #9 by 17 February 2017. Dua had her first top 10 hit. The song stayed in the charts for 25 weeks and had made double platinum sales by May 2021.

The early singles (2015-2017)

Dua Lipa in the Rai studios on the occasion of the presentation of her second single 'Be the One' in the television program Che tempo che fa. Milan (Italy), 2016.

Dua Lipa MWAH

Dua Lipa performs during Global's Make Some Noise Night, held at Supernova, at Victoria Embankment Gardens, London 2016.

The early singles (2015-2017)

Hotter Than Hell - May 2016

The tropical house-inspired dance track Hotter Than Hell provided Dua's first entry into the UK chart where it peaked at #15.

She wrote it herself, alongside members of the British band Ritual, and it was the third pre-release from her forthcoming eponymous debut album. While its predecessor, Last Dance, hadn't troubled the charts following its release in February 2016, this one was Dua's first notable success and put her on the music industry's map.

It became one of the sounds of summer 2016 - a catchy track delivered in the husky low voice which was already becoming her trademark feature - Hotter Than Hell has moody verses with lyrics taunting an ex-lover, all set to a pulsating beat. As well as reaching #15 in the UK, the single made the top 20 in several international markets.

'Lyrically, Hotter Than Hell was exactly what I wanted it to be,' Dua said in an interview with The New York Times. 'When I think of artists I love, like J. Cole, it's the storytelling that grabs me. I want to be honest with my music.

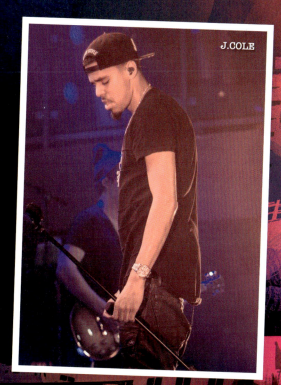
J.COLE

"This guy just made me feel like I wasn't good enough, always kicking me down in a way emotionally. And I was in the mood to write a really sad song. But when I started writing lyrics I was like, "Oh, I don't want to let him hear how he made me feel." I didn't want to show weakness — that's not what I wanted to portray. And I was like: "Ok, I'm going to flip the script. I'm going to make it seem as if he couldn't get enough of me." And instantly, the second I started writing, I started feeling better about the situation because I went into this imaginative world where everything had changed.'

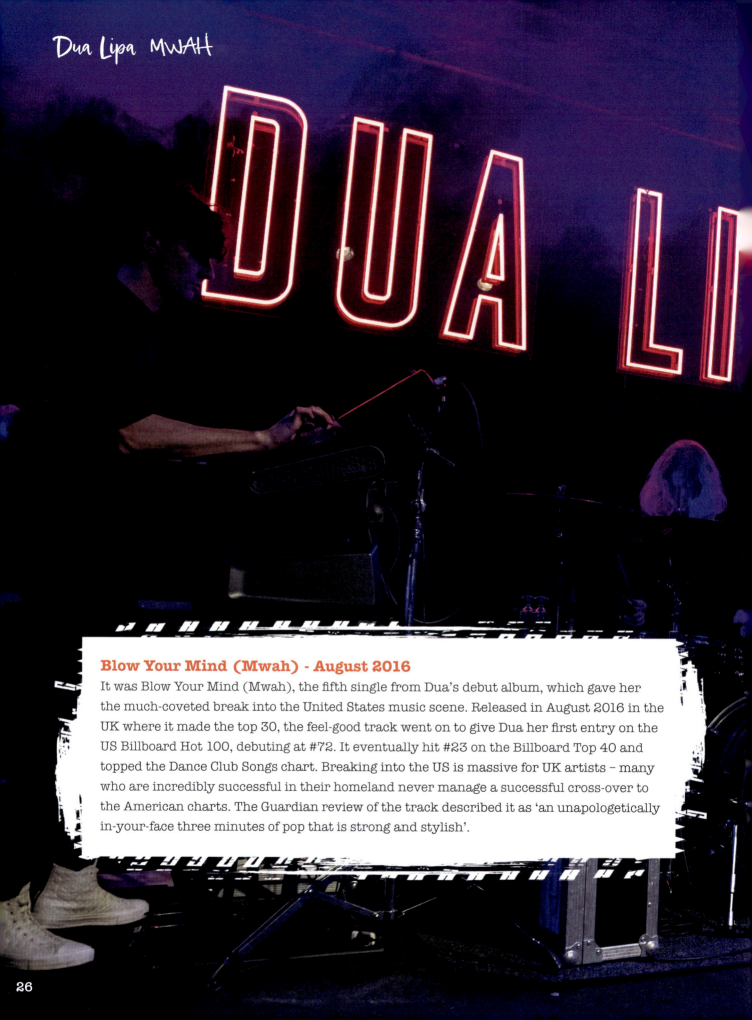

Blow Your Mind (Mwah) - August 2016

It was Blow Your Mind (Mwah), the fifth single from Dua's debut album, which gave her the much-coveted break into the United States music scene. Released in August 2016 in the UK where it made the top 30, the feel-good track went on to give Dua her first entry on the US Billboard Hot 100, debuting at #72. It eventually hit #23 on the Billboard Top 40 and topped the Dance Club Songs chart. Breaking into the US is massive for UK artists – many who are incredibly successful in their homeland never manage a successful cross-over to the American charts. The Guardian review of the track described it as 'an unapologetically in-your-face three minutes of pop that is strong and stylish'.

Dua Lipa performs at the Tunnel club in Milan, Italy 2016.

Dua Lipa MWAH

Dua Lipa performs onstage during Wireless Festival at Finsbury Park, London, 2016.

The early singles (2015-2017)

BELOW: At the SWR3 New Pop Festival, Baden-Baden, Germany, 2016.

BOTTOM: Dua being interviewed for 4MUSIC, 2016.

Dua Lipa MWAH

No Lie – November 2016
Sean Paul featured Dua on his hit single No Lie in November 2016 which reached number 10 in the UK chart. Influenced by R&B, reggae and tropical, this party pop song was about being attracted to a girl in a club. It was Dua's first UK top 10 single and did well all over Europe.

The early singles (2015-2017)

Dua Lipa with Sean Paul at Capital's Jingle Bell Ball at the O2 Arena in London, 2016.

Scared to Be Lonely (with Martin Garrix) – January 2017

The Scared to Be Lonely collaboration with Martin Garrix peaked at No.14 in the UK. Although it wasn't officially linked to an album at the time, the duet was a commercial success and made the top 10 in 12 countries, including #3 in Holland and Sweden, #9 in Germany and #10 in Belgium. In the UK and New Zealand it reached #14 and made #76 on the US Billboard Hot 100. The song has continued to grow in popularity and five years after its original release, has gone platinum or higher in 15 territories and triple platinum in Garrix's home country, the Netherlands. By February 2022 the song had been streamed a billion times on Spotify, the sixth time for Dua and the second for Garrix to hit that milestone. Speaking about his decision to use Dua on the track, Garrix said; 'I already worked on several demos for this track and I was looking for the right vocalist. When I heard Dua's version of the song I was blown away.

'It's important for artists to be recognisable through their voice so that when you hear them on the radio you think, "Oh that's Dua Lipa!" She has that for sure'.

Dua lipa with Martin Garrix perform on stage at the British Summer Time Festival in Hyde Park, London, 2017.

The early singles (2015-2017)

Dua Lipa performing live at Space 15 Twenty for Urban Outfitters Music, in Hollywood, LA, California, 2017.

Dua Lipa MWAH

Lost in Your Light (ft Miguel) April 2017

Dua's 2017 collaboration with new wave R&B singer Miguel opened up a whole new genre for her. Interviewed by HMV.com, Dua said; 'I love Miguel, he's always been at the top of my list of people that I wanted to work with. So I reached out to him and asked if we could try something together and he agreed. We wrote Lost in Your Light together and it was such fun, it came together really organically and we've become good friends.' The dance track features lyrics all about being deeply in love with another person, to the exclusion of everything else in life.

Dua Lipa performs on stage at the BBC Radio 1 Teen Awards, 2017 at Wembley Arena, London.

The early singles (2015-2017)

Dua's dazzling debut album (2017)

As Dua became increasingly successful with singles such as Hotter than Hell and Blow Your Mind (Mwah), her life started to change. As well as beginning to make music award nomination lists, she was in demand as a cover girl, and, most satisfyingly for her, was selected as a featured artist on tracks by leading producers and artists that she truly admired. Her work with Sean Paul on No Lie and with Martin Garrix on Scared to Be Lonely brought the plaudits she deserved at last. In February 2017 both those songs were in the top 15 of the UK singles chart, alongside her own Be the One. She was a long way past covering other people's songs; now she was the person to cover.

After six years of hard work and promotional build up, six huge hit singles, three of which had made the UK Top 40, and two years spent writing and recording in the studio, Dua released her highly anticipated debut album Dua Lipa on 2 June 2017. It had been delayed twice (from an original release date of September 2016, then February 2017) in part to allow the inclusion of what were described as 'exciting collaborations'. The wait had evidently been worth it as the album immediately became the biggest selling week one female solo debut in the UK that year, entering the chart at #5.

SEAN PAUL

RIGHT: Dua awarded the ASCAP Vanguard Award for 'recognition of the impact of new and developing musical genres, which help shape the future of music', 2017, in London.

Dua's dazzling debut album (2017)

Dua explained the self-title as being because, '...this album is me. It's a pure representation of who I am as a person and as an artist'.

The album's lyrical themes revolve around Dua's personal views of love, sex and self-empowerment. In an interview with Digital Spy, Dua spoke about wanting to be 'as truthful as possible' with this record, saying;

> 'I want people to see a piece of me. I want people to have an insight into everything that's happened over the last few years while I was writing the album and actually really get to know me'.

Encompassing dance and electro pop and R&B genres, the album was front-loaded with her dancefloor hits to date, but also included the delicate, piano-backed acoustic ballad Homesick, co-written by Coldplay's Chris Martin; Garden, a sweeping, soulful number, and the emotional No Goodbyes. She demonstrated she could handle understated songs just as well as she belted out a banger.

Of the 25 songs included on all editions of Dua Lipa, Dua co-wrote 21. Many of the songs were produced by Stephen 'Koz' Kozmeniuk, but other producers and songwriters were also involved, including Digital Farm Animals who produced Be the One.

The striking album cover was a beautiful shot of Dua staring into the camera, shaded with purples and blues. The deluxe version was the same shot with different background colours of pink and green, while the Complete Edition, issued in 2018, was the same again but with added glitter.

CHRIS MARTIN

Dua Lipa MWAH

After a further surge in sales following Dua's performance at the February 2018 Brit Awards, the album went on to reach #3 on the UK albums chart. It also made the top 10 in several other countries, including Belgium, Ireland, the Netherlands, Sweden, Australia and New Zealand. By October 2018 it had become the most streamed album by a female artist on Spotify. In the US, the album made its debut at #86 on the Billboard 200, eventually peaking at #27. Boosted by the issue of the Complete Edition, it spent a total of 97 weeks on the chart.

Dua's career went to another level just a few weeks after the album's release when the track New Rules was released as a single and became a global hit, getting to #1 in the UK and peaking at #6 in the vital US market. This single was an absolute gamechanger. The follow up IDGAF was also a massive hit.

DUA LIPA

RELEASE DATE: June 2017

RECORD LABEL:
Warner Bros. Music

TRACK LIST:
Genesis
Lost in Your Light Ft Miguel*
Hotter Than Hell*~
Be the One*~
IDGAF*~
Blow Your Mind (Mwah)*~
Garden
No Goodbyes*
Thinking 'Bout You
New Rules*~
Begging*
Homesick*

Recorded between 2015-17, it ran at 40 mins 43 seconds and featured a total of nine singles (denoted with *) including five which made the UK Top 40 (denoted with ~).

The original 12-track Dua Lipa was re-released in October 2018 as a super-deluxe ('Complete' edition) containing 13 additional tracks including three previously unreleased songs and past collaborations where Dua had provided vocals including Calvin Harris's chart-topping hit One Kiss and the Martin Garrix single Scared to Be Lonely:

Dreams
Room for 2
New Love
Bad Together
Last Dance
Want to
Running
Kiss and Make Up (with BLACKPINK)
One Kiss (with Calvin Harris)
Electricity (with Silk City)
Scared to Be Lonely
 (with Martin Garrix)
No Lie (with Sean Paul)
New Rules (Live)

Dua's dazzling debut album (2017)

Dua, winner of Best British Solo Artist at the BBC Radio 1 Teen Awards 2017 at Wembley Arena, London.

Dua's dazzling debut album (2017)

what the critics said

NME

NME said her debut album, '… doesn't so much hint at Dua Lipa becoming a superstar as scream it from the rooftops', before going on to describe it as 'a sass-packed, honest, uncompromising storm…. And before the Chris Martin-penned closing track 'Homesick', there isn't a standard ballad within sight. No dull moments, not a whiff of boring, just bangers ….a record that won't rest until it's compressed every available hook into gigantic pop songs.'
* * *

ALL MUSIC

'With the confidence and determination of a seasoned vet, English-Albanian singer/songwriter Dua Lipa crafted a delightful collection of catchy pop gems where the songs only serve to highlight her vocal prowess. The second half of the LP shines an extra spotlight on Lipa's voice, which, to some extent, can echo the control and power of Adele and Sia …an excellent first effort from a budding pop star.'
* * *

THE GUARDIAN

'…a solid pop debut that is high on summery nonchalance.'
* * * * *

NEW YORK TIMES

'….a mash up of tempos and pop R&B vibes.'

Dua Lipa MWAH

The album was promoted by Dua's third official headlining concert tour. Called 'The Self-Titled Tour,' it kicked off in Brighton on 5 October 2017, taking in over 20 countries and lasting over a year.

By the end of 2017, Dua had got herself noticed by everyone in the industry who mattered. As well as releasing a knockout album and bestriding the charts with its hit singles New Rules and IDGAF, she had appeared at the prestigious Glastonbury Festival, where she pulled one of the biggest crowds of recent times.

She was also beginning to win big awards. On the back of her early hits and European concert appearances, she had already won the Public Choice prize at the European Border Breakers Awards. She'd also been named Glamour magazine's 2017 Next Breakthrough Artist.

Then, she picked up the NME's Best New Artist Award 2017 - beating a strong field including Blossoms, Christine and The Queens and Zara Larsson in the process. The judges said that her sound was '...built to be spilling out of tents and clubs across Europe'.

That would happen sooner rather than later ....

TOP RIGHT: Dua winner of the Next Breakthrough award, attends the Glamour Women of The Year Awards 2017 in Berkeley Square Gardens, London.

BOTTOM RIGHT: Dua collecting her award for Best New Artist during the VO5 NME Awards 2017 held at the O2 Brixton Academy, London.

MAIN IMAGE: Dua performing during the Glastonbury Festival at Worthy Farm in Pilton, Somerset, 2017.

Dua's dazzling debut album (2017)

'I want to have a long career. I never want it to stop. I know I only get one chance at this and I want it to be the best it can be. It means so much to me'.

GLASTONBURY 2017

Dua declared this appearance to be a career highlight at that time. The crowds sang back every note as Dua belted out banger after banger from the sassy IDGAF to the more soulful Lost in Your Light. 'It was really, really special,' Dua said of the gig. 'The crowd was amazing and I had the best time'.

SET LIST FOR THE JOHN PEEL STAGE, 23 JUNE 2017

Hotter Than Hell
Dreams
No Lie
Lost in Your Light
New Rules
IDGAF
Blow Your Mind (Mwah)
Genesis
No Goodbyes
Begging
Scared to Be Lonely

Dua Lipa MWAH

Dua's dazzling debut album (2017)

Dua at Capital FM's Summertime Ball at Wembley Stadium, London, 2017.

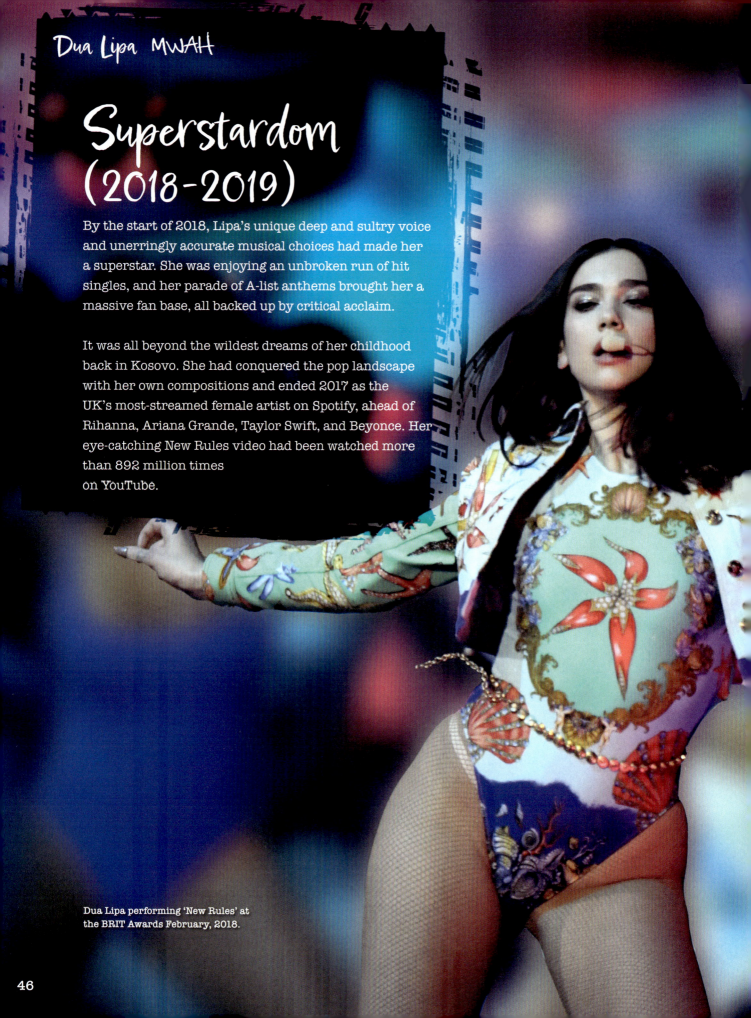

Dua Lipa MWAH

Superstardom (2018-2019)

By the start of 2018, Lipa's unique deep and sultry voice and unerringly accurate musical choices had made her a superstar. She was enjoying an unbroken run of hit singles, and her parade of A-list anthems brought her a massive fan base, all backed up by critical acclaim.

It was all beyond the wildest dreams of her childhood back in Kosovo. She had conquered the pop landscape with her own compositions and ended 2017 as the UK's most-streamed female artist on Spotify, ahead of Rihanna, Ariana Grande, Taylor Swift, and Beyonce. Her eye-catching New Rules video had been watched more than 892 million times on YouTube.

Dua Lipa performing 'New Rules' at the BRIT Awards February, 2018.

Superstardom (2018-2019)

ARIANA GRANDE

TAYLOR SWIFT

RIHANNA

In January 2018, she made history at the Brit Awards when she was nominated in five categories, including best album, becoming the first female artist ever and the only artist that year, to achieve that many nominations. 'How is this real?' she tweeted at the time. At the ceremony in London on 21 February, she went on to win the awards for 'British Female Solo Artist' and 'British Breakthrough Act' and also performed her female empowerment anthem New Rules, which had been the sound of the previous summer.

Superstardom (2018-2019)

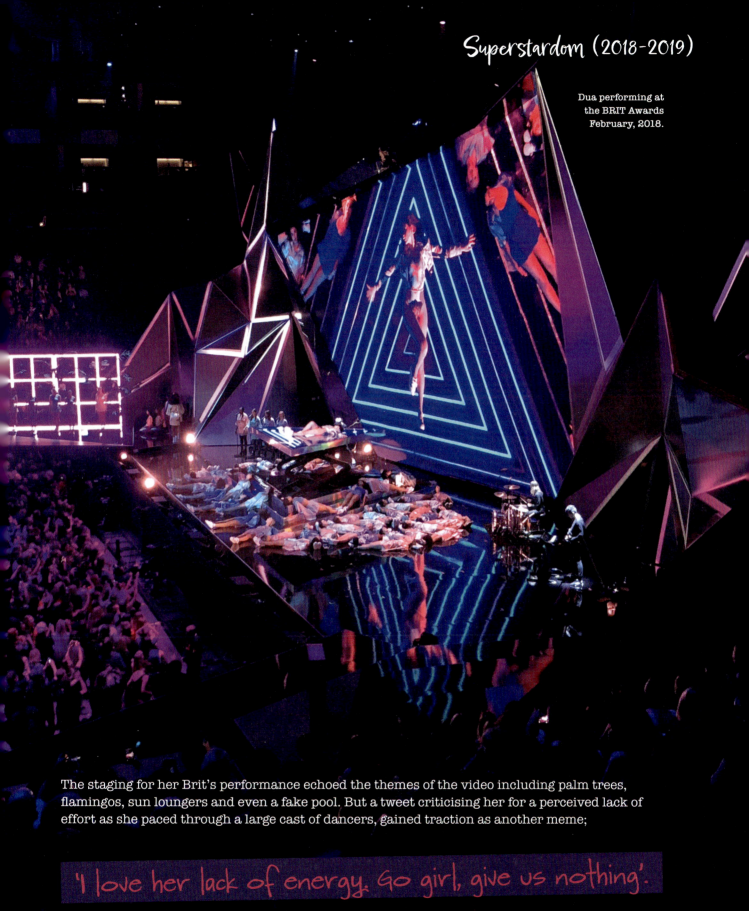

Dua performing at the BRIT Awards February, 2018.

The staging for her Brit's performance echoed the themes of the video including palm trees, flamingos, sun loungers and even a fake pool. But a tweet criticising her for a perceived lack of effort as she paced through a large cast of dancers, gained traction as another meme;

'I love her lack of energy. Go girl, give us nothing'.

Dua Lipa MWAH

While negative social media activity is best ignored, for once Dua took notice and was inspired to improve her live performances. She had dropped into the Brits midway through her 14-month 'The Self-Titled Tour' and had been understandably short of time to rehearse.

'It's one thing when people are mean about you, but you know you did your best,'

Dua told Vanity Fair.

'But it's another thing when people are mean about you and you know that you actually haven't had the opportunity to be the best because you've spread yourself so thinly in trying to do everything at once.'

According to Vanity Fair, Dua mentioned the 'nothing' comment specifically.

'You want to show that you're here to stay and you want to show that it's not just about one album or one big song or whatever it is, I just wanted to make sure

Superstardom (2018-2019)

Dua Lipa performing at the BRIT Awards February, 2018.

that this time around, I was very much in control of the fact that I'm going to do the music, then I'm going to rehearse. And then when I come in and I do the performances, they're all going to be amazing. I'm going to prove to people that I can do this and that I'm here to stay'.

Dua Lipa MWAH

And in another move set to further silence criticism, she followed up by adding another huge dimension to her career, achieving parallel success as a collaborator and guest vocalist for some of the biggest names in the business.

In April she worked with Calvin Harris on his incredibly catchy huge hit single One Kiss which topped numerous dance and electronic charts and gave Dua her second #1 in the UK. After staying at the top of the charts for eight consecutive weeks, One Kiss went on to become the biggest selling UK song of the year.

Dua's second outstanding collaboration of 2018 came in September when she featured on Electricity, which was released by Silk City, a new 'super duo' comprising music producers Diplo and Mark Ronson.

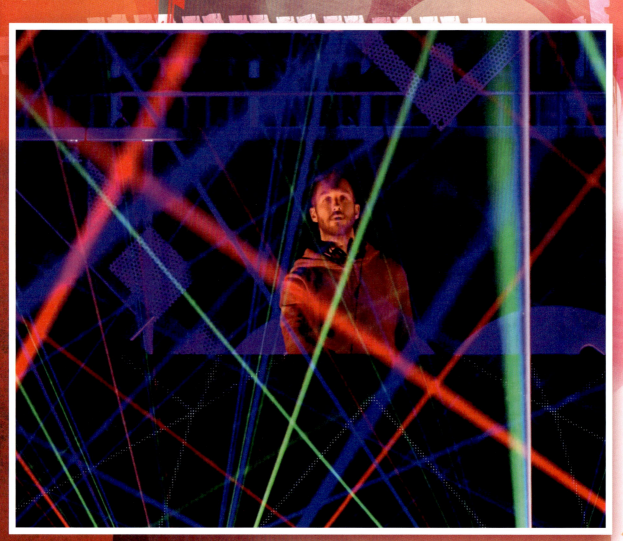

Superstardom (2018-2019)

2018 HIGHLIGHTS

Dua Lipa was the most-streamed female artist in the UK and the second most streamed globally on Spotify.

Her song One Kiss, with Calvin Harris, was the second most-streamed track of the year on Spotify, after Drake's God's Plan.

The self-titled debut album Dua Lipa was the third most-streamed record in the UK, and the fourth globally, on Spotify.

ABOVE: English-American musician, DJ, songwriter and record producer Mark Ronson and American DJ and record producer Diplo and the new 'Superduo'.

LEFT: Scottish DJ, record producer, singer, and songwriter Calvin Harris.

Dua Lipa MWAH

2019 got off to a sparkling start, perfectly illustrated by Dua's appearance on the cover of the January issue of fashion bible British Vogue.

Dua was chosen as the cover star for Vogue's special 'Future Issue' dedicated to the revolution that a new generation of talent was bringing about in the fashion industry and beyond. In his introduction to the issue, Editor in Chief Edward Enninful described Dua as a 'global superstar ...a remarkable game changer'. The stunning photograph of Dua dressed in feathery white was notable for having been taken by Nadine Ijewere, the first black woman ever to shoot a Vogue cover.

Then in February came huge professional validation in the form of major awards.

The biggest prize in music is a Grammy award and, on 10 February at the awards ceremony in Los Angeles, Dua picked up two. Her first came when 'Electricity', her collaboration with Silk City, won the 'Best Dance Recording' category. It was a huge honour but came early in the evening when she was rehearsing for her performance later in the show, so she didn't get to accept it on stage.

Dua arriving for the 61st Annual Grammy Awards Los Angeles, California, 2019.

Superstardom (2018-2019)

Dua appears backstage with her awards for Best New Artist and Best Dance Recording for 'Electricity,'.

Dua Lipa MWAH

But then, later in the evening, she was on stage and visibly stunned to pick up the prize for 'Best New Artist'. In an understandably emotional acceptance speech, Dua thanked her fans, her family and her team and said that her win should serve as an inspiration for anyone hoping to achieve success without letting go of who they are. She said that:

> '...anyone who doesn't realise how special they are to have a different story, a different background or a name that honours their roots... just know that no matter where you are from or your background, or what you believe in, never let that get in the way of you and your dreams because you deserve it, and I'm proof that you can do whatever you put your mind to'.

Dua received more professional recognition just days later when she figured among the big winners at the Brit Awards on 20 February, taking home, with Calvin Harris, the prize for 'Best Single' with One Kiss. She had been nominated for a total of four awards, making her the most nominated artist for the second year running and meaning that she effectively beat herself in the best single category where she was also nominated for IDGAF.

Superstardom (2018-2019)

The BRIT Awards winners! Calvin Harris and Dua Lipa backstage, London.

Dua has since said that these massive award wins in 2019 made her determined to work even harder, feeling some pressure to live up to them and believing that they pushed her to make more music that she was really proud of, and which felt authentic to her.

She was already busy writing new material. Throughout the hectic work schedule of the previous year, Dua had been working on her second album. The stakes were high – would she be a one album hit wonder or was she on the road to long term success as a career artist?

Dua Lipa MWAH

'In my head I was like, ok, now I need to prove that this isn't just a one off thing'.

Superstardom (2018-2019)

Cannes Gala, 2019.

Dua Lipa MWAH

Future Nostalgia

Second albums are tricky affairs for most artists, especially when their debuts have been a hit. Should they mimic that first success? Or try something different? While there is a certain amount of security attached to 'sameness', Dua was determined to carve out a fresh creative path and give her album a cohesive dance-pop aesthetic. That involved ignoring the pressures and opinions of others in an industry that tends to foster the 'if it ain't broke don't fix it' maxim. As she told the New York Times, if she hadn't done so '...I knew I would be stuck in a studio trying to make another "New Rules". That's a vicious cycle where I don't grow and nobody else benefits from that because it's just the same song again and again, and I just don't want to'.

For her second album, the title came first. Dua describes it as 'a lightbulb moment' which happened when she was in Las Vegas and the words 'future nostalgia' came to her. 'I just had the feeling of wanting it to be very reminiscent and nostalgic something that touches on inspiration and the music that I listened to my whole life, but also very current'.

She texted her manager who loved the name and agreed that Dua should just go with it, get in the studio and see what came. She teamed up with previous collaborators including Koz, Sarah Hudson and Clarence Coffee Jr for sessions in London and Jamaica.

> 'No ballads, only bangers' was the brief from the start.

The team would often kick off their writing time by playing around with tarot cards to get everyone talking, and then further inspiration came as Dua shared the lyrics and ideas which had come to her since they had last got together. One such topic was space and an intergalactic feeling of love. An image of Dua driving a car in space would eventually become the image for the album cover. During another session the team ordered a delivery of doughnuts to give them some energy – and the result was the smash single Levitating. The story goes that the whole team began riffing on the back of the resulting sugar rush. Koz played a track, Dua started making up the melody and they wrote the song pretty much all in one voice note, including the word 'sugarboo' a nickname they used for each other.

Dua also found herself tuned into tracks made with analogue synths which seemed bespoke, rather than computer synths which could be more easily replicated.

Future Nostalgia (2020)

Describing the resulting album as 'disco-orientated' and '[feeling] like a dancercise class', Dua further detailed her inspiration for the album saying; 'What I wanted to do with this album was to break out of my comfort zone and challenge myself to make music that felt like it could sit alongside some of my favourite classic pop songs, whilst still feeling fresh and uniquely mine. I was inspired by so many artists on the new record from Gwen Stefani to Madonna to Moloko to Blondie and Outkast, to name just a few. Because of the time that I'd spent on the road touring with my band, I wanted Future Nostalgia to have a lot more of a live element but mixed together with modern electronic production. My sound has naturally matured a bit as I've grown up, but I wanted to keep the same pop sensibility as I had on the first record. I remember that I was on my way to a radio show in Las Vegas thinking about the direction for this new record and I realised that what I wanted to make was something that felt nostalgic but had something fresh and futuristic about it too'.

BLONDIE

MOLOKO

Joe Kentish, Head of A&R at Warner Records UK, who originally signed Dua, explained more about the conception of Future Nostalgia in an interview with MusicBusinessWorldwide.com. 'Dua had the idea that it was going to be big, live and referencing her icons. At the time there were no disco records in the charts; there were no records doing what she did.'

Describing his reaction when he first heard Levitating he said,

'It was a 'Eureka!' moment — a contemporary lyric, but with this old school thing and still feeling modern. And that set the tone for the rest of the album'.

Dua performs at the American Music Awards in Los Angeles.

Dua Lipa MWAH

One big difference between her debut and this follow up was the different place that Dua inhabited mentally. 'When I was creating the first album a lot of what was going on in my life was about heartbreak,' she told Rolling Stone. 'This time round I was feeling so happy, and things were going so well, I was like, ok I need to portray this feeling in a way that doesn't feel cheesy to me. There was a point where I was like, oh everybody loves a ballad, maybe I should make one. But that wasn't what I was feeling. I was like '***k it – It's a fun record. That's what it is.'

She put the record on ice after it was finished so she could concentrate on her choreography.

'On my first record, I was learning everything as I went," she says. 'This time round, I knew I wanted to finish my record and then I really wanted to get into the performance side of it, make sure I had enough time for rehearsal, make sure I made every performance unique. I knew what I had to do to be the very best I could be, so I made sure I had a significant amount of time to be able to do that.'

The lead single, Don't Start Now was released on 31 October 2019 and the second single Physical followed on 30 January 2020. Both were huge hits and heralded the likely success of the whole album's release.

Scheduled to launch in April 2020 on the back of a platinum debut album, six platinum singles and a host of performances around the world, the buzz around Future Nostalgia was huge. Album releases are generally well choreographed events, particularly for an album as eagerly anticipated as this second offering from Dua, so naturally everything was in place. Then disaster struck. The mechanics of her album roll out fell apart as the world effectively closed down to get through the global health crisis caused by the Covid-19 virus.

With Glastonbury cancelled and Dua's 85-date arena tour rescheduled, she and her team considered cancelling the album release until things had settled down; although of course nobody knew when that would be. The decision was eventually taken out of their hands when the album leaked online. Dua, the great planner and strategist, had for once been wrong footed and had to act quickly to regain some control. The main question was should she, and could she, officially launch during a pandemic? The situation was unprecedented. There was so much upset in the world at that time, and her album was particularly upbeat, with not even one ballad among its track list.

Other artists, including Lady Gaga and Sam Smith, did delay their imminent album launches, but Dua decided to carry on. She announced the release of her album live on Instagram, 11 days before the previously scheduled launch date. Sitting in quarantine in an Airbnb (having found her own London flat flooded when she'd returned from Australia for lockdown) Dua found herself in the unexpected position of promoting her album online from a temporary home.

Future Nostalgia (2020)

Clearly upset, with her face half covered by her hand, she said, 'I really didn't want to do this. I've been a little bit conflicted about putting music out and you know, whether it's the right thing to do during this time because lots of people are suffering'.

She composed herself and went on to explain that she had assembled a dancey, upbeat album that made her feel good. She hoped especially now that it would bring her fans a bit of joy at a very uncertain time.

There was undoubtedly an element of risk in releasing an album of dancefloor bangers when no one could actually have a night out. 'I was terrified,' Dua told Rolling Stone afterwards, 'But at the same time I was like, for some people this is a form of escapism'.

That's certainly how things turned out.

Instead of getting lost amid the pandemic, her collection of up-tempo bangers proved just what her fans needed in lockdown. And her lyrics like "Don't show up/Don't come out" and "I should have stayed at home" took on a whole new meaning and became quarantine memes.

Although it had been produced for the dance floor, Future Nostalgia became the soundtrack to 'twerking in your dining room' as Dua later described it on the US TV chat show 'Jimmy Kimmel Live', as people looked for ways to entertain themselves at home. It was a fantasy nightclub concept for a world where the actual night clubs had been forced to close. Yet because every song on the album is a bop, it fitted the lockdown time perfectly. Ultimately, Dua told the BBC, it was better to set the record free instead of worrying about the 'perfect' release strategy.

'Yes, it was made to be listened out in the clubs and at festivals,' she said. 'But at the same time, I wanted to give people some happiness during this time, where they don't have to think about what's going on and just shut off and dance. Maybe it had to just come out now, rather than later.'

Luckily, audiences agreed that Dua's new music was exactly what they needed and the album was a triumph. It marked a change in sound for the singer, encompassing a 1980s/disco influenced sound including more live instrumentation. Dua had taken a unique theme and executed it brilliantly, adding a modern take to an 80s, synthy retro-sound. She

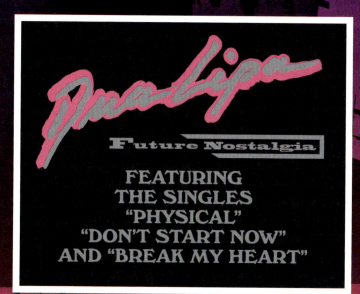

Dua Lipa MWAH

had co-written every track, collaborating with some of her favourite songwriters and producers from her debut, working alongside new artists including Tove Lo and Julia Michaels.

'It was a little bit of a sucker punch,' Dua's long-time collaborator Mark Ronson said in Rolling Stone magazine. 'I don't think anybody was expecting Dua to deliver the great cohesive pop record of 2020, but there was a sonic cohesion in the way that Random Access Memories, or The Suburbs or a Frank Ocean record feel cohesive – records that were made to sit together so people will buy it and digest it like that. And it hit right at the moment of lockdown.'

Future Nostalgia received universal acclaim and a high score of 88 on Metacritic, the website that aggregates reviews. Dua became the most listened-to female on Spotify - and the third most streamed artist on the planet – in the week of the album's release. Future Nostalgia went on to become the most streamed album by a woman, and fifth most streamed album overall on Spotify in 2020. Dua herself ended 2020 as the fourth most streamed female artist globally, behind Billie Eilish, Taylor Swift and Ariana Grande.

FUTURE NOSTALGIA

RELEASE DATE: 27 March 2020   **RECORD LABEL:** Warner Bros. Music

TRACK LIST:

- Future Nostalgia
- Don't Start Now
- Cool
- Physical
- Levitating
- Pretty Please
- Hallucinate
- Love Again
- Break My Heart
- Good In Bed
- Boys Will Be Boys
- Fever (with Angle)

In August 2020, Dua worked with DJ/producer The Blessed Madonna on a remix including contributions from BLACKPINK, Mark Ronson, Madonna, Missy Elliott and Gwen Stefani. In February 2021 came another version of Future Nostalgia - The Moonlight Edition - which included three new singles and collaborations with Miley Cyrus, J Balvin, Bad Bunny, Tainy and JID.

Future Nostalgia (2020)

Reviews

Future Nostalgia was pretty much universally lauded. Here's what the critics said:

The New York Times

'A polished trip through several eras of dance music; disco's groovy pulse, new wave's punchy synths, the brash colours of the 1980s New York club-kid house music'. The album was the perfect soundtrack to a night out – something sadly impossible as by the time the record came out most listeners were locked down in their homes.'

The Guardian

'Britain's biggest female star tightens her grip on the crown with a viscerally brilliant second album …The 11-track Future Nostalgia offers neither features nor filler, and makes a strident case for Lipa as a pop visionary, not a vessel…an outlandishly great second album'.

All Music [Re The Moonlight Edition]

'Not a moment is wasted here, and Future Nostalgia is a brisk and breathless experience that begs to be played on loop. With an endless supply of confidence, charm, and cooler-than-you attitude, Lipa pulls listeners onto the dancefloor with immediate earworms like the funky kiss-off Don't Start Now, the rapturous out-of-body rave Hallucinate, and the glistening full-body workout Physical. Flipping her hair at detractors with a wink and a smile on [the track] Future Nostalgia she sings, 'You want a timeless song/I wanna change the game'. With this flawless effort, she manages to achieve both. Future Nostalgia could have just as well been titled 'Future Classic'.

Rolling Stone

'Future Nostalgia is a breathtakingly fun, cohesive and ambitious attempt to find a place for disco in 2020'.

NME

'Lipa has long been known as an outspoken artist, standing up for what she believes in, including women's rights. The female experience is one which colours 'Future Nostalgia' from start to finish, be that through a sense of empowerment or observations on the inequality women face. "No matter what you do, I'm gonna get it without ya / I know you ain't used to a female alpha," she asserts on the title track. The confidence in her voice gives you no reason to doubt her'.

Future Nostalgia (2020)

Dua Lipa MWAH

Smash Hit Singles

New Rules - July 2017

New Rules – the shiny, house-inflected lead track from her debut album - catapulted Dua to global fame and gave her a first #1 in her UK homeland, making her the first female solo artist to do so since Adele in 2015. The track also made #6 on the Billboard 100 in the US. All of Dua's childhood dreams had come true, and her career took off into the stratosphere.

The multi-platinum song became a killer breakup anthem with its cautionary four-step plan to help avoid backsliding into a relationship with an ex. Its message of female empowerment chimed with the times and the accompanying video in which Dua's 'girl squad' support her during a slumber party is now iconic and helped propel the song to even greater success. The video clocked up 2.3 million views within 24 hours of its release and when it hit 1 billion views in February 2019 – just 223 days later – Dua became the youngest solo female artist to have reached the billion mark. It went on to receive 2.2 billion views by summer 2022, making it the 11th most-watched female music video in history.

The track has gone on to be streamed 1,710 billion times – the 38th most streamed track ever on the Spotify Top 100 and the most streamed song by a British female in the UK. It was nominated for British Single of the Year and Best British Video at the 2018 Brits and Song of the Year at the 2018 MTV Video Music Awards. The song is certified multi-platinum in 13 territories, including quadruple platinum in the UK.

IDGAF - January 2018

The MNEK-produced kiss-off "IDGAF" is another perfect track for anyone getting over a break-up. Dua's second female solidarity anthem, IDGAF had a singalong quality which helped it surge up the charts to peak at #3 in the UK and reach the top 10 in several other countries.

MNEK

Smash Hit Singles

One Kiss – April 2018

In April 2018, Dua provided vocals and contributed lyrics on the 2018 Calvin Harris banger One Kiss. The track was a phenomenal hit – it spent eight weeks at the top of the UK singles chart, giving Dua her second UK #1, going on to be the year's longest-running number one single by a solo female, as well as winning the 2019 Brit Award for Song of the Year.

It made number 76 on the Spotify Top 100 most streamed songs list with 1,465 billion streams.

Electricity – September 2018

Dua at the BRIT Awards 2019.

This dancefloor smash hit collaboration between Dua and British/American duo Silk City won Best Dance Recording at the 2019 Grammy Awards. It spent 20 weeks in the UK singles chart, peaking at #4, and 10 non-consecutive weeks on the US Billboard Hot 100, gaining platinum certification.

Don't Start Now – October 2019

The disco-inspired lead single from second album Future Nostalgia was Don't Start Now, with a tight bass line and synthesised strings underpinning Dua's husky vocals. NME described the 'banger' as 'powerful pop perfection ….a kind of counterpart to 'New Rules' that finds her delivering instructions to an ex: "Don't show up/Don't come out/Don't start caring about me now".'

It reached #2 in the UK and US, and #4 on the US year-end chart and was the most commercially successful song by a female artist in the US in 2020. Subsequently it provided Dua with her highest ranking on the Spotify Top 100 most streamed songs list, coming in at #18 with 1,954 billion streams.

Dua Lipa MWAH

Physical – January 2020

Heavily referencing the disco and electronica sound which was so prevalent in the 1980s, the aerobics/pop Physical was the second single from Future Nostalgia. It debuted at #60 on the US Billboard Hot 100 and was promoted with a colourful video with nods to the aerobic exercise workouts popular the 1980s.

Un Día (One Day) – July 2020

The line-up with Dua for this single reads like a who's who of Latin music legends. It was a collaboration including Colombian singer J Balvin and Puerto Rican superstars singer Bad Bunny and producer Tainy, who all also have writing credits. Featuring on the best of 2020 year-end lists published by Billboard, Rolling Stone and Idolator, the track went multi-platinum in the US, Mexico and Spain, as well as reaching the top 10 in various Central American countries.

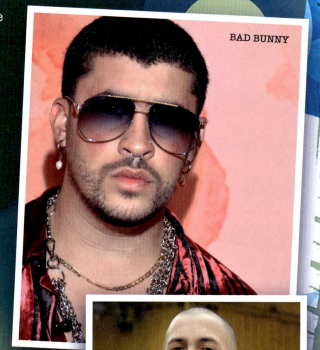

BAD BUNNY

TAINY

Levitating – October 2021

This euphoric electro-disco single was a smash-hit, making history as the longest-ever charting Billboard Hot 100 hit from a female solo artist where it spent 70 weeks and became the top title of 2021. It beat How Do I Live by LeAnn Rimes from 1997/98 to become only the fifth single ever to spend at least 70 weeks on the Billboard chart since its inception in 1958 and made number 84 on the Spotify Top 100 most streamed songs list with 1,428 billion streams.

Dua has credited the song as being key to shaping the whole of her Future Nostalgia album. She also described getting so excited about it in the studio that the recording session became an impromptu party. The 'outer space' references which pervade the album include the idea of 'levitating' when falling in love.

It was written by Dua with Clarence Coffee Jr, Sarah Hudson and Koz, who also produced alongside Stuart Price.

Smash Hit Singles

29th Annual Elton John AIDS Foundation Academy Awards Viewing Party, 2021.

Cold Heart - August 2021

In what Elton John described as the 'culmination of a beautiful friendship', he worked with Dua and Australian dance trio Pnau to produce the chart-topping hit Cold Heart (Pnau remix) as the lead single for his album 'The Lockdown Sessions'. The slick mash up of Elton's classic hits borrows heavily from his 1989 hit Sacrifice, and 1972's Rocket Man, and includes elements from 1976's Where's the Shoorah? and 1983's Kiss the Bride. It was released as a single alongside an animated music video and was a huge hit, providing Dua with her third #1 in the UK, and giving Elton his first #1 in 16 years, and 8th overall. It was also a hit in the US where it peaked at #7. In July 2022 the track joined Spotify's 'billions' club – meaning that it amassed over 1 billion streams on their service.

Dua Lipa MWAH

Owning lockdown

Digital music and platforms had already changed the way people consumed music, but everything went to another level during the Covid lockdowns.

Adaptation was key and, ever the innovator, Dua was quick to push herself to find a way to promote her music and engage with her fans while the world was in retreat and traditional concerts were not possible.

She began to perform over Zoom, for example singing what was then her forthcoming single, Don't Start Now, from her living room on James Corden's Late Late Show. 'Honestly, this Zoom session rivals the production quality of some music videos we've seen,' praised US digital entertainment site Wrap News Inc.

Owning lockdown

She also collaborated with Elton John on the huge hit track Cold Heart, produced for his Lockdown Sessions album. Reportedly, Elton reached out to Dua during the pandemic lockdowns to discuss a remote collaboration.

> 'She's given me so much energy. She's a truly wonderful artist, and person, absolutely bursting with creativity and ideas'.

For her part, Dua said she was 'honoured and privileged' to collaborate with him. The accompanying music video, created by animator and illustrator Raman Djafari, showed animated versions of Elton and Dua entering a euphoric world, then being separated as their planets drifted away from each other in a reference to the way people were kept apart during their time in lockdown.

In her real life, when she wasn't working, Dua told interviewers that she had gotten through lockdown by spending time cooking, reading... and thinking of even bigger and better performance ideas – including a virtual show.

Once it became clear that the whole of 2020 would be a write-off as far as live concerts were concerned, Dua came up with the idea of forming a 'bubble' with other musicians and back up dancers for a live virtual show to be streamed for fans.

Called Studio 2054, as a nod to the legendary Studio 54 New York nightclub of the 1980s, Dua's show went live on 27 November 2020 and immediately set a live-stream record as more than five million people tuned in. Having been starved of live performances during the months of lockdown, viewers lapped up the high-definition details, flashy sets, sleek choreography and glittery line up of stars including Miley Cyrus, Elton John and Bad Bunny.

Sponsored by American Express, the show cost a reported US$1.5 million to stage and was an incredible feat for the time. While also paying homage to the Future Nostalgia universe, it recreated the club culture Dua's

MILEY CYRUS

LEFT: Homefest, James Corden's Late Late Show Special, 2020.

Dua Lipa MWAH

fans were missing and improved the view most people would have from their seat in an arena. As well as various songs from Future Nostalgia, the show included a new unreleased track with FKA Twigs and old favourites such as New Rules, One Kiss and Electricity.

FKA TWIGS

On the back of Future Nostalgia, Dua was nominated for six Grammys, including Album of the Year, Song of the Year, Record of the Year and Best Pop Solo Performance. On the night of the intimate, masked and socially distanced Grammy awards ceremony on 14 March 2021, Dua went on to pick up the award for Best Pop Vocal album, beating Justin Bieber's Changes, Lady Gaga's Chromatica, Harry Styles' Fine Line and Taylor Swift's folklore.

The award crowned a triumphant period in Dua's life. Future Nostalgia had peaked at number one on the Official UK Albums Chart in April 2020, while four of the album's singles entered the top ten of the Official Singles Chart. At the time of the album's release, Lipa became the first English female artist since Vera Lynn in 1952 to have three top-ten singles in the chart at the same time.

All that had been missing was the chance to get out and perform for her fans – and that was something she was working on and determined to do at the very earliest opportunity. Despite her worldwide success and continuing career accolades, Dua was subject to the same restrictions as the rest of the population and couldn't take her hit album on tour until the world opened up again.

Owning lockdown

Dua, winner of the award for best pop vocal album for "Future Nostalgia," at the 63rd annual Grammy Awards in Los Angeles.

Dua Lipa MWAH

Owning lockdown

Reviews of Studio 2054

ROLLING STONE
'A smashing success'

NME
'A big night in with a pop great'

VARIETY
'The post-thanksgiving dopamine rush we all needed'

DAILY TELEGRAPH
'The best I have seen'

Graham Norton Show, 2020.

Dua Lipa MWAH

The tours

Dua first toured in 2016, before she had an album to promote. While it's unusual for a new artist to tour before ever releasing an album, it made perfect sense for Dua. She was a genuine talent, unfiltered and not manufactured by a label. Her singles had made a huge impact and were strong enough to carry a concert. She also had the chance to support acts including Kevin Garrett, The 1975 and Troye Sivan.

Dua performing live onstage during the European leg of her 2017 US and Europe Tour.

'You've gotta work really, really hard — not just for music, but for anything you do in life'.

Dua Lipa

The tours

In 2017 she supported Bruno Mars on his '24K Magic World Tour', as well as enjoying a summer of festival appearances, alongside promotion of her forthcoming debut album. By the end of the year, once her album had become a hit, she set off on another series of dates on her 'The Self-Titled Tour'. During this tour she was supported variously by Off Bloom, Grace Carter, Marteen, Lauv and The Chainsmokers. Dua herself opened for Coldplay on dates in Brazil and Argentina during the band's 'Head Full of Dreams' tour.

Dua stayed on the road for the whole of 2018, playing a string of arena and theatre shows supported variously by Tommy Genesis, Eves Karydas, Vic Mensa, Col3trane, Clairo and Yoshi Flower. She also took time out to support Bruno Mars again in Australia. In total she gave 245 live shows while promoting her Dua Lipa album – a huge achievement at that stage of her career which she has since celebrated by having the number 245 tattooed onto the back of her left arm.

Discussing Dua's commitment and work ethic, TaP Management's Ben Mawson has said that she 'puts in the time and she cares about countries which are difficult to make a mark in'. He cited China which was challenging, and a place she visited several times while promoting her first album. During a concert in September 2018 during which some of her fans were ejected by security guards at the National Exhibition and Convention Centre for dancing and apparently waving flags in support of gay rights, Dua told the audience, 'I want to create a really safe environment for us all to have fun...I want us all to dance. I want us all to sing. I want us all to just have a really good time.' Later she tweeted; 'I will stand by you all for your love and beliefs and I am proud and grateful that you felt safe enough to show your pride at my show. What you did takes a lot of bravery. I always want my music to bring strength, hope and unity. I was horrified by what happened and I send love to all my fans involved.'

Understandably, in 2019, she eased off what had been a punishing performance schedule and played just 15 times, mainly at award shows and festivals. Then in 2020, she only had the opportunity to perform three times before the world went into lockdown and all live shows were cancelled.

So her 2022 Future Nostalgia tour was massively anticipated by fans desperate to experience her latest album live.

As well as having a chance to dance their socks off at a Dua show, her fans know they will see stunning performances too. Dua has a clear sense of the visual – which means her live shows are off the scale. While she has obviously grown in confidence and gained vast experience since her early days on stage, she still gets scared before a live show. She says that her knees are physically shaking from the mix of adrenaline and excitement, adding; 'It's scary but I love doing it'.

Dua Lipa MWAH

2016 UK Tour
Dates (excluding TV and award show appearances)

JANUARY 2016
- 16   Louisiana, Bristol, UK
- 17   The Hope & Ruin, Brighton UK
- 26   O2 ABC, Glasgow, UK
- 27   Soup Kitchen, Manchester, UK
- 29   Sunflower Lounge, Birmingham, UK
- 30   Stealth, Nottingham, UK

FEBRUARY 2016
- 2   Oslo, Hackney, London, UK

MARCH 2016
- 17   St Cecilia Hotel, Texas, USA
- 18   Hype Hotel (SXSW showcase), Texas, USA
- 31   Heaven, London, UK

APRIL 2016
- 2   G-A-Y, London, UK
- 27   538 Koningsdag Festival, Breda, Netherlands

MAY 2016
- 4   Baby's All Right, New York, USA *
- 5   McKittrick Hotel, New York, USA
- 9   School Night (showcase) Bardot, Los Angeles, USA
- 27   Dot to Dot Festival, Manchester, UK
- 28   Dot to Dot Festival, Bristol, UK
- 29   Dot to Dot Festival, Nottingham, UK

JUNE 2016
- 26   Glastonbury Festival, Worthy Farm, Pilton, UK

JULY 2016
- 8/10   Wireless Festival, Finsbury Park, London, UK
- 13   Newtown Social Club, Sydney, Australia
- 14   Northcote Social Club, Melbourne, Australia
- 21/24   Secret Garden Party Festival, Milton Keynes, UK
- 29   House of Blues, Chicago, USA **
- 30   Lollapalooza Festival, Grant Park, Chicago, USA

AUGUST 2016
- 3   Mercury Lounge, New York, USA
- 6   Brighton Pride, UK
- 10   Sheshi Nënë Tereza, Tirana, Albania
- 14   Flow Festival, Helsinki, Finland
- 17   Pukkelpop Festival, Hasselt, Belgium
- 18   FM4 Frequency Festival, Green Park, Austria
- 19/21   Lowlands Festival, Netherlands
- 25   Zürich Openair Festival, Zürich, Switzerland
- 26   Stars for free, Chemnitz Arena, Germany

SEPTEMBER 2016
- 3   Energy Air Festival, Stade de Suisse, Switzerland
- 16   Music Midtown Festival, Piedmont Park, Georgia, USA

* supporting Kevin Garrett
** supporting The 1975

2016 Hotter Than Hell Tour
Dates

OCTOBER 2016

5	The Academy, Dublin, Ireland
7	Gorilla, Manchester, UK
10	Koko, London, UK
12	Café de la Danse, Paris, France
14	Ancienne Belgique, Brussels, Belgium
15	Paradiso, Amsterdam, Netherlands
17	Lille Vega, Copenhagen, Denmark
19	Heimathafen Neukölln, Berlin, Germany
20	Mojo Club, Hamburg, Germany
22	Die Kantine, Cologne, Germany
24	Gibson, Frankfurt, Germany
25	Backstage Club, Munich, Germany
28	Tunnel, Milan, Italy

NOVEMBER 2016

3	Lakewood Civic Auditorium, Ohio, USA***
4	Stage AE, Pittsburgh, Pennsylvania, USA***
5	EXPRESS LIVE! Ohio, USA***
7	The Fillmore Detroit, Detroit, USA***
8	REBEL, Toronto, Canada***
10	MTELUS, Montréal, Canada***
12	Agganis Arena, Boston, USA***
13	Iridium, New York, USA
14/15/16	Terminal 5, New York, USA***
17	Eagle Bank Arena, Fairfax, Virginia, USA***
18	The Tabernacle, Atlanta, Georgia, USA***
26	Free Radio Live, Genting Arena, Birmingham, UK

DECEMBER 2016

2	O2 Institute, Birmingham, UK
3	Capital FM Jingle Bell Ball, O2 London, UK
4	Top of the Pops Christmas and New Years Specials, Elstree Studios, UK
16	Metro Radio Christmas Live, Newcastle, UK
17	Radio City Christmas Live, Liverpool, UK
23	The Flame, Flanders, Belgium

***supporting Troye Sivan on his Suburbia Tour

Dua Lipa MWAH

2017 US and Europe Tour Dates

FEBRUARY 2017
24 Lincoln Hall, Chicago, USA
25 The Shelter, Detroit, USA
27 Mod Club Theatre, Toronto, Canada

MARCH 2017
1   Irving Plaza, New York City, USA
2   The Foundry at the Fillmore, Philadelphia, USA
4   Paradise Rock Club, Boston, USA
5   Rock & Roll Hotel, Washington DC, USA
7   The Loft, Atlanta, USA
8   The Social, Orlando, USA
9   State Theatre, St Petersburg, Florida, USA
11 House of Blues, Houston, USA
12 Prophet Bar, Dallas, USA
14 Crescent Ballroom, Phoenix, USA
15 The Belasco, Los Angeles, USA
17 Great American Music Hall, San Francisco, USA

APRIL 2017
5   Fabrique, Milan, Italy
7   Columbia Theater, Berlin, Germany
8   Luxor, Cologne, Germany
9   TivoliVredenburg, Utrecht, Netherlands
12 O2 Ritz, Manchester, UK
13 O2 Shepherd's Bush Empire, London, UK
19 Space 15 Twenty, Los Angeles, USA
20 Jimmy Kimmel Live, Los Angeles, USA
27 538 Koningsdag Festival, Breda, Netherlands

MAY 2017
3   The One Show, London, UK
17 Intimate Showcase, Warner Music Indonesia, Jakarta, Indonesia
28 BBC Radio 1's Big Weekend, Hull, UK

JUNE 2017
2/3 The Governors Ball, Randall's Island Park, New York, USA
9   MTV Live at ExCel, London, UK
10   Summertime Ball, London, UK
11   Bonnaroo Music & Arts Festival, Tennessee, USA
17   KFEST, Bethel Woods Center, New York, USA
18   Kiss the summer hello, Canalside, Buffalo, New York, USA
18   Canalside Buffalo, New York, USA
23   Glastonbury Festival, Worthy Farm, Pilton, UK
24   B96 Pepsi Summer Bash, Allstate Arena, Illinois, USA
28   Open'er Festival, Poland
29   Rock Werchter, Flanders, Belgium

JULY 2017
2   Barclaycard British Summer Time, Hyde Park, London, UK
3   Montreux Jazz Festival, Switzerland
6   House Festival, Marble Hill House, London UK
8   Balaton Sound, Zamárdi, Hungary
13-16 Festival Internacional de Benicàssim, Valencia, Spain
14-16 Longitude Festival, Dublin, Ireland
18   Ibiza Rocks Hotel, Ibiza, Spain
29   Europa Plus Live, Moscow, Russia

AUGUST 2017
4   MEO Sudoeste, Portugal
12   Good Vibes Festival, The Ranch, Kuala Lumpur, Malaysia
13   WE THE FEST, Jakarta, Indonesia
17   In The Mix, SM Mall of Asia Arena, Philippines
20   Summer Sonic, Osaka, Japan
24   Reading Festival, UK

The tours

SEPTEMBER 2017

2	Energy Music Tour, Berlin, Germany
5	The Qube, Amsterdam, Netherlands
14	Spectrum Center, Charlotte, North Carolina, USA ****
17	Music Midtown, Atlanta, Georgia, USA
20	Value City Arena, Ohio, USA ****
21	YouTube Space, New York, USA
22-24	Life is Beautiful Festival, Las Vegas, USA
23	Madison Square Garden, New York, USA ****
26	Prudential Center, New Jersey, USA ****
27	KeyBank Center, Buffalo, New York, USA ****
28	iHeartRadio Theater, New York, USA
29/30	Capital One Arena, Washington DC, USA ****

'It's actually really crazy to think that, at 15, I was uploading covers to YouTube, and now I'm walking onstage at Shepherd's Bush Empire in my hometown. This is everything I could possibly have dreamt of, and yeah, it's nuts. If I was telling 15-year-old me that I'd be doing this, right now? I'd probably have a really big giggle'.

Dua speaking to YouTube in 2017

****supporting Bruno Mars on his 24K Magic World Tour

Dua Lipa MWAH

The Self-Titled Tour – 2017/18

Leg 1 – Europe

OCTOBER 2017

5	Brighton Dome, Brighton, UK
6	O2 Academy, Bournemouth UK
8	O2 Academy, Leeds, UK
10	Manchester Academy, Manchester, UK
11	O2 Academy, Glasgow, UK
13	O2 Academy, Newcastle, UK
14	O2 Academy, Birmingham, UK
17	Yoyo (Palais de Tokyo) Paris, France
19	Backstage Club, Munich, Germany
20	Batschkapp, Frankfurt, Germany
21	Rockhal, Esch-sur-Alzette, Luxembourg
24	Live Music Hall, Cologne, Germany
25	Astra Kulturhaus, Berlin, Germany
27	Docks, Hamburg, Germany
29	Rockefeller Music Hall, Oslo, Norway
30	Münchenbryggeriet, Stockholm, Sweden

NOVEMBER 2017

1	Amager Bio, Copenhagen, Denmark
3	Lotto Arena, Antwerp, Belgium
5	AFAS Live, Amsterdam, Netherlands
6	O2 Academy Brixton, London, UK

Leg 2 – South America

NOVEMBER 2017

8	Allianz Parque, São Paulo, Brazil *****
9	Audio Club, São Paulo, Brazil
11	Arena de Grêmio, Porto Alegre, Brazil *****
13	Teatro Vorterix, Buenos Aires, Argentina
14/15	Estadio Cuidad de La Plata, Buenos Aires, Argentina *****

***** opening for Coldplay on their Head Full of Dreams Tour

Leg 3 – North America and Europe

NOVEMBER 2017

19	Festival Corona Capital, Mexico City, Mexico
20	House of Blues, Boston, USA
22	REBEL, Toronto, Canada
23	MTELUS, Montréal, Canada
24	Hammerstein Ballroom, New York, USA
26	Aragon Ballroom, Chicago, USA
28	The Fillmore Silver Spring, Maryland, USA
30	The Cannery Ballroom, Nashville, USA

DECEMBER 2017

2	Poptopia, SAP Center, San Jose, USA
5	Palace Theatre, Albany, USA
6	Venu Nightclub, Boston, USA
8	BBC Television Centre, London, UK
9	Capital Jingle Bell Ball, The O2 Arena, London, UK
14	Dave and Jimmy's Jingle Jam, Columbus, USA
15	The Fillmore, Detroit, USA

JANUARY 2018

30	MTELUS, Montréal, Canada

FEBRUARY 2018

5	Ogden Theatre, Denver, USA
6	The Depot, Salt Lake City, USA
8	Hollywood Palladium, Los Angeles, USA
9	The Van Buren, Phoenix, USA
10	House of Blues, San Diego, USA
12	Hollywood Palladium, Los Angeles, USA
13	SF Masonic Auditorium, San Francisco, USA
14	Jimmy Kimmel Live, Los Angeles, USA
15	Roseland Theater, Portland, USA
16	Vogue Theater, Vancouver, Canada
17	Showbox, Seattle, USA

The tours

Leg 4 - Asia
FEBRUARY 2018
24   Du Forum, Abu Dhabi, UAE

Leg 5 - Oceania
27/28   Spark Arena, Auckland, New Zealand***

MARCH 2018
2   Spark Arena, Auckland, New Zealand
3   Spark Arena, Auckland, New Zealand***
7/8/10/11   Rod Laver Arena, Melbourne, Australia***
12   Palais Theatre, Melbourne, Australia
20   Qudos Bank Arena, Sydney, Australia***
21   Big Top Luna Park, Sydney, Australia
22   Palais Theatre, Melbourne, Australia
23/24   Qudos Bank Arena, Sydney, Australia***
26   Adelaide Entertainment Centre, Adelaide, Australia***
28/29   RAC Arena, Perth, Australia***

Leg 6 - Europe
APRIL 2018
9/10   Olympia Theatre, Dublin, Ireland
12   OVO Hydro, Glasgow, Scotland
14/15   O2 Apollo, Manchester, UK
17   The Resorts World Arena, Birmingham, UK
18   Motorpoint Arena, Cardiff, Wales
20   Alexandra Palace, London, UK,
24   Annexet, Stockholm, Sweden
29   Baku Crystal Hall, Baku, Azerbaijan

Leg 7 - Asia
MAY 2018
1   MacPherson Stadium, Hong Kong
3   KL Live, Kuala Lumpur, Malaysia
4   The Star Theatre, Singapore
6   Yes24 Live Hall, Seoul, South Korea
8   Zepp Toyko, Japan
20   MGM Grand Garden Area, Las Vegas, USA

Leg 8 - Europe
JUNE 2018
1   Orange Warsaw Festival, Warsaw, Poland
2   Crocus City Hall, Moscow, Russia

Leg 9 - North America
JUNE 2018
5   Revention Music Center, Houston, USA
6   South Side Ballroom, Dallas, USA
9   Coca-Cola Roxy, Atlanta, USA
10   Bonnaroo Music & Arts Festival, Tennessee, USA
11   Revolution Live Outdoors, Fort Lauderdale, Florida, USA
12   Klipsch Amphitheater at Bayfront Park, Miami, USA
13   House of Blues, Orlando, USA
16   WBLI Summer Jam, Wantagh, New York, USA
17   Kiss Concert, Xfinity Center, Massachusetts, USA
19   98.5's Summer Smash, F.M Kirby Center, Pennsylvania, USA
20   Toyota Oakdale Theatre, Wallingford, USA
21   Kiss the summer hello, Canalside, Buffalo, New York, USA
23   B96 Summer Bash, Rosemont, Illinois, USA

***supporting Bruno Mars on his 24K Magic World Tour

Dua Lipa MWAH

The tours

The Self-Titled Tour 2018

Dua Lipa MWAH

24	Minneapolis Armory, Minneapolis, USA
26	The Fillmore, Denver, USA
28	The Chelsea, Las Vegas, USA
29	Cal Coast Credit Union Open Air Theatre, San Diego, USA
30	Bill Graham Civic Auditorium, San Francisco, USA

JULY 2018

2	WAMU Theater, Seattle, USA

Leg 10 – Europe

JULY 2018

4	Le Consulat, Paris, France
6	Nrj in the Park, Parc du Vissoir, Trélazé, France
7	Roskilde Festival, Denmark
8	Ruisrock Festival, Turku, Finland
10	Glasgow Green, Glasgow, Scotland***
12	Stavern Festival, Larvik Golf Arena, Norway
14	Mad Cool Festival, Valdebebas-IFEMA, Madrid, Spain
21	Tomorrowland Festival, Boom, Belgium
22	Lollapalooza Festival, Paris, France

Leg 11 – North America

JULY 2018

27	Panorama NYC, Randall's Island Park, New York, USA
30	RBC Echo Beach, Toronto, Canada

AUGUST 2018

4	Lollapalooza Festival, Chicago, USA
5	Osheaga Festival, Parc Jean-Drapeau, Montréal, Canada

Leg 12 – Europe and Asia

AUGUST 2018

10	Sunny Hill Festival, Germia Park, Pristina, Kosovo
12	Sziget Festival, Budapest, Hungary
14	Regnum Carya Hotel, Antalya, Turkey
15	Pukkelpop Festival, Hasselt, Belgium
19	Lowlands Festival, Netherlands
25	Reading Festival, UK
26	Leeds Festival, UK

SEPTEMBER 2018

1	Electric Picnic, Stradbally Hall, County Laois, Ireland
3	Sugarcity, Halfweg, Netherlands,
9	Lollapalooza, Berlin, Germany

Leg 13 – Asia

SEPTEMBER 2018

11	Sun Yat-sen Memorial Hall, Guangzhou, China
12	NECC Arena, Shanghai, China
14	Mall of Asia Arena, Manila, Philippines
16	Formula 1 Grand Prix, Marina Bay Street Circuit, Singapore
17	GMM Live House, Bangkok, Thailand
19	Taipei International Convention Center, Taipei, Taiwan

Leg 14 – North America

SEPTEMBER 2018

22	iHeartRadio Festival, Las Vegas Festival Grounds, Las Vegas, USA
27	The Chelsea, Las Vegas, USA
30	Toyota Oakdale Theatre, Wallingford, USA

NOVEMBER 2018

30	KIIS FM Jingle Ball, Inglewood, USA

***supporting Bruno Mars on his 24K Magic World Tour

The tours

DECEMBER 2018
- 2   iHeartRadio Jingle Ball, Toronto, Canada
- 5   Jingle Ball, Philadelphia, USA
- 7   Madison Square Garden, New York, USA
- 10   The Fillmore Auditorium, Denver, USA
- 12   iHeartRadio Jingle Ball, Allstate Arena, Illinois, USA
- 20   OVO Arena, Wembley, London, UK

The Future Nostalgia Tour

With the massive Future Nostalgia tour delayed because of the Covid-19 pandemic, fans had to wait two years after its release to experience Dua's live performance of the album. She did not disappoint. Reflecting the album's disco influenced, up-tempo exercise class vibe, Dua had barely a second to breathe when she was on stage.

Dates
Leg 1 - North America

FEBRUARY 2022
- 9   FTX Arena, Miami, USA
- 11   Amway Center, Orlando, USA
- 12   State Farm Arena, Atlanta, USA
- 14   Bridgestone Arena, Nashville, USA
- 16   Spectrum Centre, Charlotte, USA
- 18   TD Garden, Boston, USA
- 19   Wells Fargo Centre, Philadelphia, USA
- 21   UBS Arena, Elmont, USA
- 23   Fiserv Forum, Milwaukee, USA
- 25   Little Caesars Arena, Detroit, USA
- 26   Schottenstein Center, Columbus, USA

MARCH 2022
- 1   Madison Square Garden, New York, USA
- 2   Capital One Arena, Washington, USA
- 4   Prudential Center, Newark, USA
- 5   KeyBank Center, Buffalo, USA
- 8   Target Center, Minneapolis, USA
- 9   United Center, Chicago, USA
- 12   Toyota Center, Houston, USA
- 13   American Airlines Center, Dallas, USA
- 15   Ball Arena, Denver, USA
- 17   BOK Center, Tulsa, USA
- 20   Footprint Center, Phoenix, USA
- 22/23   The Forum, Inglewood, USA
- 25   T-Mobile Arena, Las Vegas, USA
- 27   SAP Center, San Jose, USA
- 29   Moda Center, Portland, USA
- 31   Climate Pledge Arena, Seattle, USA

APRIL 2022
- 1   Rogers Arena, Vancouver, Canada

Leg 2 - Europe

APRIL 2022
- 15   AO Arena, Manchester, UK
- 17   Utilita Arena, Birmingham, UK
- 18   First Direct Arena, Leeds, UK
- 20/21   3Arena, Dublin, Ireland
- 23   Utilita Arena, Newcastle, UK
- 24   OVO Hydro, Glasgow, UK
- 26   Motorpoint Arena, Nottingham, UK
- 27   Motorpoint Arena, Cardiff, UK
- 29   M&S Bank Arena, Liverpool, UK

Dua Lipa MWAH

MAY 2022
- 2/3 — O2 Arena, London
- 6/7 — Sportpaleis, Antwerp, Belgium
- 9 — Barclays Arena, Hamburg, Germany
- 10 — Mercedes-Benz Arena, Berlin, Germany
- 12 — Lanxess Arena, Cologne, Germany
- 15 — Accor Arena, Paris, France
- 17/18 — Ziggo Dome, Amsterdam, Netherlands
- 20 — Hallenstadion, Zürich, Switzerland
- 22 — Olympiahalle, Munich, Germany
- 23 — Wiener Stadthalle, Vienna, Austria
- 25/26 — Mediolanum Forum, Milan, Italy
- 28 — Unipol Arena, Bologna, Italy
- 30 — Halle Tony Garnier, Lyon, France

JUNE 2022
- 1 — Palau Sant Jordi, Barcelona, Spain
- 3 — WiZink Center, Madrid, Spain
- 5 — Altice Forum, Braga, Porugal
- 6 — Altice Arena, Lisbon, Portugal
- 21 — Žalgirio Arena, Kaunas, Lithuania
- 23 — Hartwall Arena, Helsinki, Finland
- 26 — Spektrum, Oslo, Norway
- 28 — Gröna Lund, Stockholm, Sweden

Leg 3 – North America

JULY 2022
- 25 — Bell Centre, Montréal, Canada
- 27 — Scotiabank Arena, Toronto, Canada

Leg 4 – South America

SEPTEMBER 2022
- 8 — Distrito Anhembi, Sao Paulo, Brazil
- 11 — Barra Olympic Park, Rio, Brazil
- 13/14 — Campo Argentino de Polo, Buenos Aires, Argentina
- 16 — Estadio Bicentenario, Santiago, Chile
- 18 — Parque Salitre Magico, Bogotá, Colombia
- 21 — Foro Sol, Mexico City, Mexico
- 23 — Estadio Borregos, Monterrey, Mexico

Leg 5 – Oceania

NOVEMBER 2022
- 2/3 — Spark Arena, Auckland, New Zealand
- 5 — Brisbane Entertainment Centre, Australia
- 8/9 — Qudos Bank Arena, Sydney, Australia
- 11/12 — Rod Laver Arena, Melbourne, Australia
- 14 — Adelaide Entertainment Centre, Adelaide, Australia
- 16 — RAC Arena, Perth, Australia

Haters gonna hate....

Instead of letting the Internet bring her down and stunt her growth, Dua has always tried to use criticism as a spur for improvement. A great example of this came when a dance move which involved twisting one leg was described by online haters as being the action of a pencil sharpener or looking like 'somebody trying to get their shoe on in a rush without bending down'. Hilariously, Dua has reclaimed the dance as part of her Future Nostalgia set, using it to open up with as Don't Start Now begins. 'It actually caused me a lot of grief at the time as I was being bullied online,' said Dua. 'But now on reflection I have a fondness for it, it helped me grow and I made sure I did more rehearsal'.

Incomparable Lipa's in the pink with super slick joyful show

Evening Standard review of Future Nostalgia tour London O2 show, by Gemma Samways, published 3 May 2022.

If ever an album screamed out to be experienced live it's Future Nostalgia.

Released at the height of the first lockdown, Dua Lipa's retro-leaning love letter to the dance floor provided panicked pop fans with some much-needed escapism.

But as much as we've all enjoyed shimmying around our kitchens to Don't Start Now, at the first of her two O2 arena shows Lipa proved that nothing compares to hearing these songs in person.

Now 40 dates in, the tour is intimidatingly slick. From the playlist of early Noughties handbag house preceding the show's start, to the pin-sharp moves created by Super Bowl half time choreographer Charm La'Donna, there was a sense that every detail had been pored over to ensure maximum enjoyment.

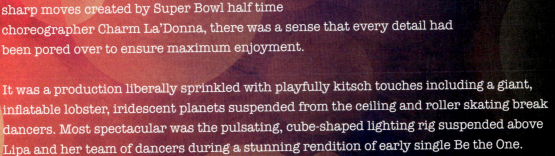

It was a production liberally sprinkled with playfully kitsch touches including a giant, inflatable lobster, iridescent planets suspended from the ceiling and roller skating break dancers. Most spectacular was the pulsating, cube-shaped lighting rig suspended above Lipa and her team of dancers during a stunning rendition of early single Be the One.

But for all the glitter showers, confetti cannons and hot pink Balenciaga, the quality of the music was the main attraction. Lipa moved from hit to hit with scarcely a pause. For such a precision-tooled performance, it was interesting that the night's most affecting moment came when Lipa deviated from the script: 'I feel like my heart is in my throat. We've waited two whole years for this moment'.

As anyone who witnessed last night's outpouring of joy will attest, it was an experience absolutely worth the wait.

ABOVE: Dua performs during the Future Nostalgia Tour at Madison Square Garden, New York, 2022.

Dua Lipa MWAH

Dua performs during the Future Nostalgia Tour.

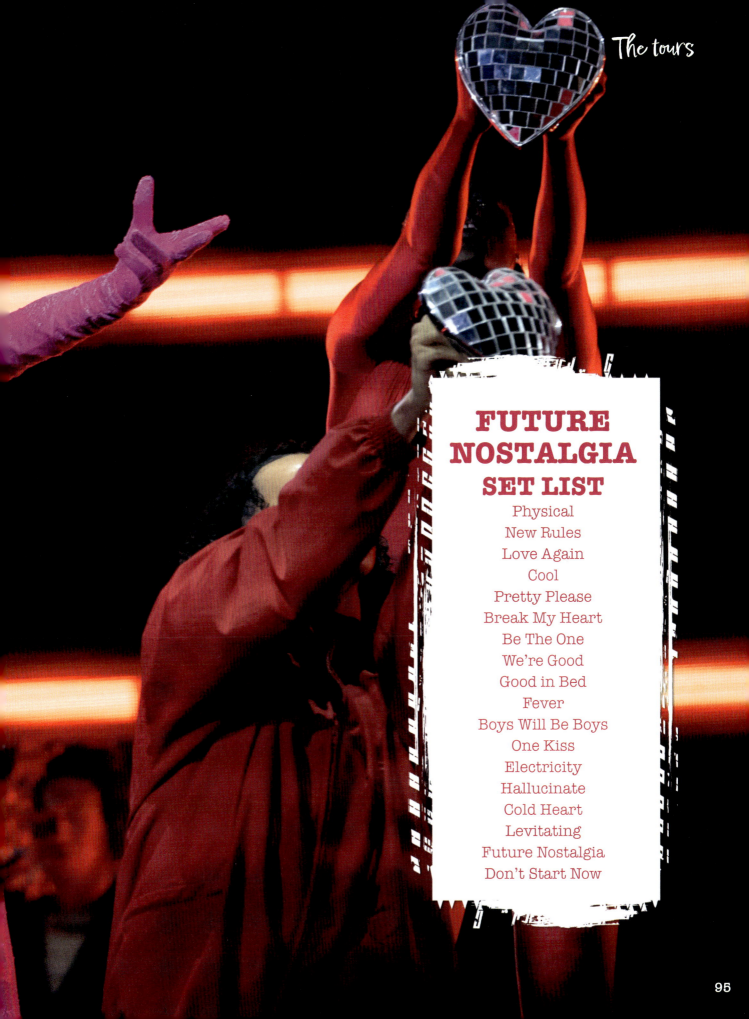

The tours

FUTURE NOSTALGIA SET LIST

Physical
New Rules
Love Again
Cool
Pretty Please
Break My Heart
Be The One
We're Good
Good in Bed
Fever
Boys Will Be Boys
One Kiss
Electricity
Hallucinate
Cold Heart
Levitating
Future Nostalgia
Don't Start Now

Dua Lipa MWAH

Dua performs during the Future Nostalgia Tour.

The tours

Skilful songwriting

Although she got noticed because of her voice and performance of covers, Dua had always wanted to write her own music. As an established singer who had grown up loving pop bangers, it was natural that she would begin to write her own.

'With my first record, I was lucky to get songs like New Rules and Be the One that I didn't write, but which were also massive parts of my career,' she said in an interview with the BBC. 'But I also felt like I had a lot to prove.'

'For a pop artist, people can see you as manufactured, and think that you just get a writing credit for turning up. But, for the songs I did write, I was in those sessions, and they are my personal experiences. And that's something I wanted to get across in every interview I did.'

By the time of Future Nostalgia, Dua had proved her credentials and knew exactly what she needed to achieve.

The result was that on this album she has a writing credit on every song. Not that she went in determined to reject other people's songs and ideas, rather she was just very inspired and clear about what she wanted to say. She told YouTube that her song writing comes from a very honest and very personal place. 'The songs that I chose to cover, I chose them because I really love them as songs. But it's different when I'm telling my own story.'

For example, the track Boys Will Be Boys includes the line, 'putting your keys between your knuckles when there's boys around' which came from Dua's personal experiences of travelling around London as a young girl. 'I remember walking home, especially in the wintertime, when I was getting off my bus and just trying to get to my flat, which was a three minute walk from the bus stop, and just being petrified of boys on bikes catcalling around the estate', she told the BBC.

She included the memory in her song because she wanted it known that she understood the everyday fears women face, and that men rarely encounter. By sharing her memory with her female fans, she hoped that they would feel seen and heard and know that all women go through the same things.

At the other extreme of a feminine perspective, Dua wrote about feeling powerful, rather than fearful, in the album's title track when she sings about getting what she wants by being a female alpha.

Skilful songwriting

> 'I'm not suggesting that's what I am, but when you can sing that song, you want to feel stronger and more empowered'.

She regularly turns an emotion on its head and imagines the scenario from an unfamiliar perspective.

'My music, a lot of it, is what I hope. I hope to empower women,' she told Rolling Stone. 'Those [words] don't immediately come from something that I believe. It's more that I start off with a false sense of confidence, and then the more I sing it, the more I perform it, the more I put it out into the world, the more I feel like I live it, breathe it, embody those lyrics and those words.'

She calls her blend of heavy beats and heavy emotions 'dance-crying,' explaining in an interview with The New York Times: 'All the sad things that happen are the things that linger on my mind the longest, the things that I feel like I want to write about. But then at the same time I like dancing to it. So it's finding that mixture between lyrically it being very personal and inspired by events, and then being able to also listen to it and dance along and not think about what the lyrics can mean.'

Remarking on Dua's talent as a song writer, Joe Kentish, Head of A&R at Warner Records UK said; 'I don't think you put together a record like Future Nostalgia as an artist unless you're an excellent writer yourself. I don't think it happens. She'd tell you herself that when she started going into writing studios it was intimidating. That was something I tried to be aware of and responsible about – a young girl, 17 or 18, going into those environments with guys who were older, she often wasn't in control of the surroundings. Regardless of anything else, you're the rookie in the room.

'Future Nostalgia is only 11 tracks long; I would say Dua comfortably wrote at least 150 songs [for the record], ideas, jotting things down. And every one of those songs is one or two days of your life.'

THE AWARDS

AMONG MANY WORLDWIDE ACCOLADES, DUA HAS WON:

7 Brit Awards
3 Grammy Awards
1 Billboard Music Award
3 iHeartRadio Music Awards
6 Global Awards
2 American Music Awards
3 YouTube Creator Awards
2 Guinness World Records

'If you're not passionate about becoming a great writer, the process is going to become really boring, especially for someone like Dua who has many options to do so many other great things. But instead of all that, she stayed in the studio and slogged it out. That's a testament to her ambition.'

> 'You're not getting a record like this unless you have a strong narrative. And that narrative comes from her'.

Dua's former manager Ben Mawson agrees, saying, 'We've seen artists who might get half a good song out of 10 writing sessions; with Dua, one in five or one in four is a banger. She gets results out of other people as well, because her personality is so engaging, and she is so charismatic. She definitely has that special something.'

Dua's work ethic is legendary. Driven and ambitious, she's a force of nature, hardworking and a keen list maker who puts in the hours. 'I've seen her get off a plane and hit a double session,' said producer Koz Kozmeniuk. 'That's not normal. And getting thrown in a room with a million other people with three hours to write a song? It's super intimidating. But she's just relentless.'

Nowadays a new generation of aspiring and established musical artists pay their respects to Dua by covering her own compositions.

'I've heard lots of them,' she says of the covers fans post to YouTube. 'It's always really, really fun and exciting to get to watch them.'

WHAT'S IN THE NAME

During the 2018 Billboard Music Awards, American tv host Wendy Williams mispronounced Dua's name as Dula Peep, which has now stuck with fans as an affectionate nickname. Speaking on The Tonight Show, Dua told host Jimmy Fallon that she was cool with it, adding, 'I mean my whole life, my name's been a little bit difficult to pronounce …. Living in London, having a full Albanian name like Dua and people pronouncing it … I feel like I just wanted a normal name; Sarah, Hannah, Chloe, anything, I'll take it!'

Skilful songwriting

Dua performing in 2018.

DUA'S DELIGHTS
Favourite food? Something spicy
Someone she'd love to collaborate with? Iconic music artist Nile Rodgers
Secret talent? She's great at spelling – try her on 'xylophone' and 'eczema'
Childhood passion? Goosebumps – the tv show and the books

Skilful songwriting

Dua performing at the BRIT Awards 2021.

Queen of collaborations

Dua has always found collaboration with other artists to be hugely inspiring. Working with songwriters and producers who bring new sounds and ideas to the table means that Dua never stands still but is constantly improving and expanding her repertoire.

'When you are an artist where Dua is, you have access to almost everybody,' Joe Kentish from Warner Records told Music Week. 'The difficulty as an artist is learning when to say no. Because if you're going to write a record with a really tight concept and sound, it's really important that you have a tight group of collaborators working on the record to provide it with a spine.'

'That was the battle on the second record, but what makes it easier is when you've got an artist who really knows what she wants to do and is also very quick to pick up on the energies she wants to be around and the people she wants to collaborate with.'

Among Dua's key collaborators so far are:

Bad Bunny

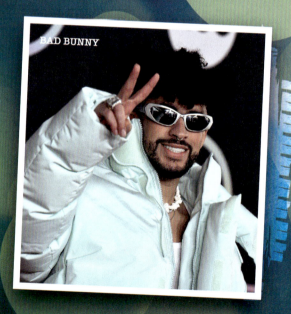

Puerto Rican rapper and singer Bad Bunny (real name Benito Antonio Martínez Ocasio) was the top global artist of 2021 – the first non-English language act to be Spotify's most streamed artist of the year (2020/2021). Known particularly for his slurred vocal style, he incorporates rock, bachata and soul styles into his Latin Trap music - a sub-genre of Latin American music incorporating Reggaeton (reggae and Latin blend) and southern hip hop styles. Like Dua, he became known online at first - uploading his music to SoundCloud before being signed. Since breaking through at the end of 2016 he has collaborated with Drake, Cardi B and J Balvin. He won the Grammy for Best Latin Pop Album in 2020, and then his third album, El Último Tour del Mundo, became the first all-Spanish album in history to top the US Billboard 200 and won him a second Grammy for Best Musica Urbana album in 2022. He's also the first Latin urban music artist to feature on the cover of Rolling Stone magazine.

Queen of collaborations

DaBaby
Grammy-nominated American rapper DaBaby (formerly Baby Jesus and real name Jonathan Lyndale Kirk) has had two consecutive Billboard 200 #1 albums, and three multi-platinum singles since breaking through in 2019. He worked on Dua's October 2020 remix of Levitating, writing a new introduction and second verse.

BLACKPINK
Record-breaking South Korean girl band BLACKPINK have made a huge impact on the Western charts.

Band members Jisoo, Jennie, Rosé and Lisa are among the biggest celebrities of K-Pop, and BLACKPINK became the first Korean girl group to enter the Billboard Emerging Artists chart and to top the Billboard World Digital Song Sales chart three times. The video for their 2018 hit single DDU-DU DDU-DU was the first by a Korean group to receive over a billion views on YouTube. Their 2020 album The Album is the best-selling of all time by a Korean group and the first to sell more than one million copies.

Their 2018 collaboration with Dua, Kiss and Make Up, made the top 40 in 19 countries including reaching #36 in the UK.

BLACKPINK

Dua Lipa MWAH

Calvin Harris

Scottish DJ, record producer and singer-songwriter Calvin Harris (real name Adam Richard Wiles) burst onto the music scene in 2007 and has since become a global superstar with album sales of over 10 million albums worldwide, including 3 million in the US and 1.7million in the UK. His 2012 hit album 18 Months topped the UK albums chart and reached #19 on the US Billboard 200. All eight singles from that album made the UK Top 10, beating the record previously held by Michael Jackson for the most UK Top 10 hits from one studio album.

His 2018 banger, One Kiss, featuring Dua Lipa, spent eight weeks at #1 and won the Single of the Year award at the 2019 Brits.

Among his many other achievements he was the first UK solo artist to reach more than one billion streams on Spotify, has 18 Brit Award nominations (winning for British Producer of the Year and British Single of the Year in 2019) five Grammy Nominations (including a win for Best Music Video in 2013) won the Ivor Novello Songwriter of the Year award in 2013 and was Top Dance/Electronic Artist at the 2014 Billboard Music Awards. He topped the Forbes list of the world's highest paid DJs every year between 2013 - 2018.

Clarence Coffee Jr

Clarence Coffee Jr is an American, Grammy-nominated songwriter and part of the award-winning songwriting and production team The Monsters & The Strangers based in Los Angeles which has credits on music from artists including Camilla Cabello, Katy Perry, Justin Bieber and Halsey.

Among his work with Dua, 'Coffee' co-wrote the massive tracks Love Again and Physical. He has said that the process of writing in Dua's team is 'very easy [because] we're not trying to do anything other than express and give something good to people'.

CLARENCE COFFEE JR

Chris Martin

Chris Martin is founder and front man of rock superstar band Coldplay, one of the most successful and best-selling music acts of all time, with album sales above 100m worldwide. Also a songwriter and instrumentalist, Chris first came across Dua when she was an up and coming artist working in a studio he visited. Impressed by her work he took a professional interest in her and gave her a song he had written, Homesick. Meeting him was a pivotal moment for Dua and helped her appreciate how she was beginning to be a force in the industry.

Queen of collaborations

Diplo

Diplo (real name Thomas Wesley Pentz) is an American house DJ, songwriter and record producer, noted for pushing music boundaries and exploring sound.

Among his many achievements he is the co-creator and lead member of the electronic dancehall music project Major Lazer, a member of the supergroup LSD, with Sia and Labrinth, one half of super-duo Silk City with Mark Ronson and partnered with Skrillex as Grammy award-winning duo Jack Ü.

As a child he was fascinated by dinosaurs and chose Diplo as his professional name as a nod to Diplodocus, which was one of his favourites.

MNEK

MNEK is the stage name of British singer, songwriter and producer Uzoechi Osisioma "Uzo" Emenike. Grammy-nominated, MNEK has worked with many of the biggest music artists in the world including Madonna, Beyonce, Kylie Minogue, Jax Jones, Little Mix, Craig David, Christina Aguilera and Selena Gomez. He was part of Dua's song writing team on her 2018 hit IDGAF.

Martin Garrix

Dutch DJ and producer Martin Garrix, also known as Ytram and GRX, worked with Dua on the EDM hit Scared to be Lonely in Feb 2017 which made the Billboard 100 EDM chart. Martin was ranked as the world's number one DJ for three years running from 2016-18 on DJ Mag's publicly voted Top 100 list. He's performed at music festivals all over the world, including Coachella, Creamfields and Tomorrowland. As well as his hit with Dua, Martin is known for his singles Animals and In the Name of Love.

GWEN STEFANI

Gwen Stefani

Multi-award winning American singer/songwriter Gwen Stefani of Hollaback Girl fame, featured on the remix of Physical for Club Future Nostalgia. She found fame as co-founder, lead vocalist and main songwriter of the 90s hit band No Doubt and, as a solo artist, with her #1 album Love. Angel. Music. Baby.

Dua Lipa MWAH

J Balvin

Colombian born Balvin is a legend in Latin music, and credited with bringing about a second generation revolution in reggaeton – a music genre which blends reggae with Latin American dance hall music and includes hip-hop influences.

He's a multi-award winning artist and songwriter, having sold more than 35 million albums and singles worldwide and won handfuls of Billboard Latin music awards, Latin Grammy Awards, MTV Video music awards, plus four Grammy nominations. He worked with Dua on Un Día and has appeared at her Sunny Hill Festival in Pristina, Kosovo.

JID

Featuring on Dua Lipa's track Not My Problem, JID (real name Destin Choice Route) is an American rapper and singer. His single Enemy with pop band Imagine Dragons boosted his career in 2021 when it peaked at #5 on the Billboard Hot 100.

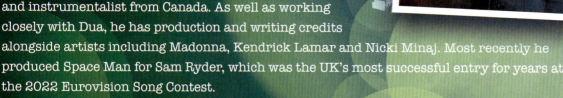

JID

Koz

Stephen Kozmeniuk, known professionally as Koz, is a Grammy-nominated record producer, songwriter, engineer and instrumentalist from Canada. As well as working closely with Dua, he has production and writing credits alongside artists including Madonna, Kendrick Lamar and Nicki Minaj. Most recently he produced Space Man for Sam Ryder, which was the UK's most successful entry for years at the 2022 Eurovision Song Contest.

Mark Ronson

British/American superstar DJ, producer and musician Mark Ronson has worked both behind the scenes and later as front man on some of the biggest and most critically acclaimed music of recent times. As well as Dua, his collaborators have included Amy Winehouse, Adele, Lady Gaga, Miley Cyrus and Bruno Mars. Ronson has won seven Grammy awards including Producer of the Year for Amy Winehouse's Back to Black album, and two for Record of the Year, one for Amy Winehouse's Rehab and the other for Bruno Mars' Uptown Funk, which is among the best-selling singles of all time, having spent 14 consecutive weeks at #1 on the Billboard Hot 100 and seven non-consecutive weeks at #1 on the UK singles chart. He also won an Oscar, a Golden Globe and a Grammy for co-writing Shallow for the 2018 film A Star is Born.

Queen of collaborations

Madonna

Long known as the Queen of Pop, there are few superlatives to add to the description of American singer/songwriter Madonna. The best-selling female recording artist of all time, with sales of over 300 million, she has sustained a phenomenal 40-year career by continually reinvented herself and breaking barriers in the music industry. She has always been a role model for Dua, not only because of her music, but also because of the way she has maintained control over her own career.

Along with Missy Elliott, Madonna was involved with The Blessed Madonna's remix of Levitating, the lead single of the remix album Club Future Nostalgia, writing new verses and a middle eight section.

Missy Elliott

American singer Missy Elliott is one of the most successful female rappers in the world, the first to be inducted into the Songwriters Hall of Fame and the winner of four Grammys. With record sales of 30 million, she has been dubbed the Queen of Rap. She found fame in the 1990s with R&B girl group Sista before going on to become a successful solo artist, with her hit debut album Supa Dupa Fly.

Miguel

American R&B singer/songwriter Miguel (Miguel Jontel Pimentel) gained commercial success with his sleeper hit album All I Want Is You in 2010. Since then he has received critical acclaim for his music which incorporates R&B, funk, hip hop and electronic styles. He worked with Dua on her 2017 track Lost in Your Light.

MIGUEL

Miley Cyrus

Former teen idol Miley who shot to fame as a singer/actress in the hit TV show Hannah Montana, is now one of the most successful female singing artists in the world. Her top five 2020 album Plastic Hearts included the single Prisoner featuring Dua, which peaked at #8 in the UK. The track was also included on Future Nostalgia: The Moonlight Edition.

Dua Lipa MWAH

Sean Paul

Sean Paul is a Grammy and Brit-nominated rapper and singer from Jamaica who featured Dua on his reggae/party track No Lie. Originally from Sean's 2018 EP Mad Love the Prequel, the song was later included on Dua Lipa: The Complete Edition, the super deluxe reissue of Dua's debut studio album.

Silk City

Super-producers Diplo and Mark Ronson teamed up as dance-pop duo Silk City in early January 2018. The American DJ and record producer, Diplo, and English/American musician, DJ, songwriter and producer Mark Ronson featured Dua Lipa on their second release Electricity in September that same year and it went on to win a Grammy for Best Dance Recording.

Sarah Hudson

American singer/songwriter Sarah Hudson is a key member of Dua's song writing team and was with her throughout the production of Future Nostalgia, including the monster hit singles Levitating and Physical.

Sarah's other huge successes include working with Katy Perry on the Billboard #1 hit Dark Horse and with Iggy Azalea and Rita Ora on the #3 Billboard hit Black Widow. She has also worked with Nicky Minaj and Little Mix.

Tainy

Tainy (real name Marcos Efraín Masís Fernández) is a Puerto Rican record producer noted for his work in the reggaeton musical genre, particularly with Bad Bunny and J Balvin. He became the number one Latin producer on the Billboard charts following the success of Balvin and Bunny's 2019 collaborative album Oasis. He co-wrote and produced the single Un Día with Dua.

DUA WITH SARAH HUDSON

Queen of collaborations

The Blessed Madonna

Famed underground American DJ, musician and producer The Blessed Madonna (formerly the Black Madonna and born Marea Stamper) also has a record label called We Still Believe.

An exciting turntablist, acclaimed for her fluent and dynamic sets, she started out in the late 1990s selling mixtapes at raves before going on to make her name in genres from disco to house to techno. She's appeared at the world's leading music festivals including Coachella and Sonar. She remixed Dua's hit Levitating, featuring American singers Madonna (no relation!) and Missy Elliott to become the fifth single from Future Nostalgia and went on to mix the 2020 album Club Future Nostalgia with guest artists including Mark Ronson, and Gwen Stefani, alongside Madonna and Missy Elliott.

Whethan

Electronic music producer and DJ Whethan (real name Ethan Snoreck) collaborated with Dua on the song High from the soundtrack of the film Fifty Shades Freed, which was released in February 2018.

Kevin Parker (Tame Impala)

The sought-after collaborator Kevin Parker is the versatile and influential mastermind behind Tame Impala. A producer and multi-instrumentalist, he has made significant contributions to contemporary music through his collaborations with various artists including Rihanna, Lady Gaga, Kanye West and Travis Scott.

Danny L Harle

British music producer and composer Danny L. Harle was closely involved with Caroline Polachek's 2019 album Pang, both as her co-writer and executive producer. He's also worked with Nile Rodgers, Charli XCX and Olly Alexander.

Going forward, Dua has said she would like to work with Nile Rodgers, Pink, Alicia Keys and Frank Ocean

Queen of collaborations

Future Nostalgia Tour 2023.

Dua Lipa MWAH

A passion for fashion

As well as her music, Dua's Instagram followers (currently numbering 88.4 million and rising) lap up information about her fashion and outfits.

Clothes have always been a passion for Dua. She has a style which is very much her own - an eclectic mix of girly and sporty – and she can be very flamboyant. Off duty she may well be seen in lowkey Adidas sweatpants, but when she is touring, Dua favours all-in-one bright sparkly outfits. 'I want fans to remember my shows by the outfits I wear, and every time I try to be different,' she says.

Costumes on her Future Nostalgia tour included a yellow catsuit, accessorised with Balenciaga opera gloves; an asymmetric body suit embellished with Swarovski crystals by Atelier Versace, and a black rhinestone corseted catsuit by Mugler – everything custom-made of course.

Whether dressed for the stage or not, she is undoubtedly a beautiful and stylish woman, although her early experiences in the modelling industry have made her determined not to trade on her looks.

'I would like to think that my voice is my best feature, I want something more like a sonic image — that someone hears it on the radio and hears my voice and thinks, instantly, that it's me. Thats more important to me that anything else'.

A passion for fashion

Dua performing in her yellow catsuit.

Dua Lipa MWAH

Nevertheless, her shiny hair, good looks and passion for fashion mean she is a much sought after cover girl. Her appearances have included front cover shots for UK, American and Turkish Vogue, Elle and British GQ. She also made the cover of the March 2021 issue of Time magazine as one of the 'future 100 most influential people in the world'.

In 2019 she became the first musician to be global ambassador for Pepe Jeans and went on to launch a capsule collection of her own with the brand. It appealed to her because she said she could remember a Pepe Jeans store in London's Portobello Road when she was a child. She signed a multi-year partnership to work with Puma as a global ambassador in November 2020 and became the face of Versace's Autumn/Winter campaign in 2021.

Pepe Jeans fashion retail store decorated with images of their global brand ambassador Dua Lipa in 2019

A passion for fashion

A long time Versace fan, Dua made her runway debut for the luxury brand in 2022, during Milan fashion week, strutting down the catwalk to the sound of her own music as tracks from Future Nostalgia played out. She opened the show wearing a black jacket and slinky side-split pencil skirt, flanked by shirtless masked men wafting archive print silk scarves.

Donatella Versace explained that she wanted Dua for her show because she had long admired the singer, and that:

> 'Right now I cannot think of a better woman to embody the spirit of Versace and of this collection.'

Dua at the Versace SS22 runway during Milan Fashion Week in September, 2021.

BELOW: Dua arriving at the Barbie European Premier wearing Versace's Summer "La Vacanza" collection campaign, co-designed by Donatella Versace and Dua.

Dua Lipa's relationship with Versace deepened further when she co-designed the brand's summer 2023 collection, La Vacanza. The collaboration with Donatella Versace resulted in a collection that perfectly captured the vibrant and playful spirit of a summer night out, and fittingly, Dua mentioned at a Cannes press conference that the idea was decided together "on a night out in New York". Signature elements like butterfly and polka dot motifs, crystal accents, and sharp tailoring make this collection the epitome of a sparklingly hot Italian summer.

Dua Lipa MWAH

Dua is regularly on the media's 'best-dressed' lists, including at the 2021 Grammy Awards when she wore a Versace dress with a butterfly effect front, and side cut outs, accessorised with Bulgari jewellery.

Probably her most famous piece of jewellery is the "Mwah" diamond choker she wore in her 'Blow Your Mind (Mwah)' video. Dua has become synonymous with the phrase and frequently blows her trademark kisses for fans with the accompanying 'mwah' sound.

She is also adorned with a number of tattoos, including the words 'Sunny Hill' on the inner of her right arm, dancing figures on each of her thumbs, a palm tree above her left elbow, the word 'angel' on her right shoulder and the phrase 'this means nothing' on her left arm, as well as the 245 number from her 2017/18 concert schedule. 'It's the idea of getting to keep something forever and having something that reminds you of a certain time and place,' Dua told Billboard. ' When I'm travelling, I feel like they ground me.'

She was glowing during appearances at the 2024 Met Gala, and on 'Saturday Night Live' to promote Radical Optimism, and when papped out and about in New York with British actor Callum Turner.

TOP: Dua wearing her diamond choker.
RIGHT: The actor, Callum Turner.

A passion for fashion

Dua at the 2024 Met Gala, New York.

A passion for fashion

Dua Lipa with Donatella Versace at Milan Fashion Week, 2022.

Making a difference

Dua is dedicated to making a positive difference wherever and whenever she can. Her message to detractors who question her involvement is 'I think people forget how small our world is. And it's getting smaller all the time'. Her Kosovan/Albanian historian grandfather reportedly lost his job when he refused to rewrite history for opposing Serbian forces, so Dua says that standing by the things she believes in is part of who she is.

She is a powerful personality, pro-Palestine, a UK Labour party supporter and an advocate for issues she cares about, including mental health and LGBTQ rights. Dua explained more about this in an interview with the UK's best-selling gay magazine Attitude, saying: 'I have a massive group of friends and [members of] my team who are part of the LGBTQ community, who have inspired me so much and taught me so much,' she said. 'They're all my role models in life. It's entirely a right to be able to love who you want, not just because I have friends in the LGBTQ community, but because we're all human and we deserve it. It's something I feel very connected to and will continue to fight for.'

In 2016, she set up the Sunny Hill Foundation in her native Pristina in Kosovo, which is focused on 'helping the Kosovan society in different aspects, especially arts and culture'. Reflecting this aim, a big part of the Foundation's fund raising effort is centred around the Sunny Hill music festival, first held in 2018.

'My dad had a crazy but amazing idea to set up a music festival,' Dua told Apple Music's Beats 1 Radio.

'I felt proud when Miley Cyrus got up and performed, she was the first international female artist to come and perform in Kosovo and put on a crazy show'.

Miley Cyrus performs at Sunny Hill Festival in Pristina, Kosovo, 2019.

Dua Lipa MWAH

Dua's father Dukagjin had long dreamed of such an event to put Kosovo on the cultural map and prove that there was more to his country than conflict. When Dua became an international star, the stage was set – she could headline the festival and bring the crowds and other world-class acts.

One of Sunny Hill Foundation's stand out projects was the reconstruction of a kindergarten which had been severely damaged by the 2019 Albanian earthquake. To raise funds, Dua co-released a limited edition line of t-shirts called 'Pray for Albania' in collaboration with Albanian fashion designers.

Dua often speaks about the importance of her roots and the fact that she channels both her Kosovan and English heritage in everything she does.

'Both places are part of me,' she says. 'So much of what I do is in twos. I like juxtapositions in my music and what I wear. I feel like my dual heritage, being from two places at once, with all of those things trickling into the other, is what makes me, me.'

She is anti-Brexit, citing the personal experience of her family: 'No refugee leaves their country without having to' she said.

Dua is direct and defiant when necessary and rarely misses a chance to point out the inconsistencies of how men and women are treated in the music industry. Famously, when accepting her 2019 Grammy as Best New Artist, she said 'I guess this year we really stepped up' – calling out Recording Academy President Neil Portnow for his comment in 2018 that female performers needed to 'step up' if they wanted fairer representation at award shows. Such plain speaking shows no sign of being silenced.

Dua arriving at The Recording Academy And Clive Davis' 2019 Pre-Grammy Gala held at The Beverly Hilton Hotel.

Making a difference

Dua Lipa MWAH

Making a difference

Dua performs on stage with her father, Dukagjin Lipa at the Germia National Park, 2016.

Dua Lipa MWAH

Radical optimism for Dua's continued success...

The phenomenal success of Future Nostalgia brought more accolades for Dua, including wins at the 2021 Brit Awards for British Female Solo Artist and British Album of the Year. She also gave a knockout performance in a mocked up and disco-fied tube train carriage at the award ceremony in May. The show had been moved on from its usual February slot because of Covid 19 restrictions and eventually took place before a live audience of people who were key workers during the pandemic lockdowns.

Dua ended 2021 as the most streamed UK artist globally, and a few months later in summer 2022, she had the top two most streamed albums by a female artist of all time on Spotify - #1 Dua Lipa and #2 Future Nostalgia.

She kicked off 2022, in a largely Covid-free world, by hitting the road at last with her delayed, but widely acclaimed, Future Nostalgia tour which ran until November when it wrapped up in Australia. But never content to rest on her laurels, Dua maintained her focus on other projects alongside her intense schedule of concert performances.

In February 2022, she launched a free weekly lifestyle newsletter called Service95, with an accompanying podcast 'Dua Lipa: At Your Service' – both available in 11 languages and curated by herself.

She describes the venture as providing a 'global style, culture and society concierge service' for people who are interested in art, music, fashion, and activism. 'I find huge joy in telling people what I've learned about in any given city and love finding connection in our shared experiences,' she says. 'Service95 takes that idea and brings it to anyone who's as curious as I am about life.'

Another 2022 highlight came in August when Dua and her father Dukagjin were both made Honorary Ambassadors of their home country, Kosovo. The titles were awarded by the country's Madam President Vjosa Osmani. 'It's an honour and a privilege to be able to represent my country all over the world and to continue my work and efforts globally to see that we leave our mark and make a difference,' said Dua in her thank you speech.

MADAM PRESIDENT VJOSA OSMANI

Radical optimism for Dua's continued success...

In common with many other people, Dua found that the Coronavirus pandemic and various lockdowns during 2020 and 2021 made a significant impact on her. In particular, her music career was limited and went off in many different directions. 'For two years we were frozen,' she said. 'I didn't get to really do these songs in the way that I'd envisioned them, and now that I've been able to put a show around it, it feels new to me.'

'But there are also ways I feel I'm moving on a little bit. Especially now that I've started writing again and working on new music.'

> 'I've definitely grown up. Overall, whether it's sonically or in terms of the themes, I've matured. It's like I'm coming into my power and not afraid to talk about things. It's about understanding what I want'.

One thing she decided she wanted in the post-Covid world was new management. Just a few days after her Future Nostalgia tour started post-lockdown in February 2022, it was reported that Dua had parted ways with Ben Mawson and Ed Millet's TaP Management and that her father Dukagjin would represent her interests until, and if, new management was appointed.

A year later, TaP Music sold the publishing rights back to her and wished Dua all the best for the future.

Her future was bright. Still with her father as her manager, Dua had begun work on her highly anticipated third studio album Radical Optimism. It was eventually released on 3 May 2024 – over four years since Future Nostalgia - so her fans had had a fairly long wait between albums, but Dua had been busy!

Dua Lipa MWAH

She actually started writing new material for the album during her Future Nostalgia tour. Then there had been the not insignificant matter of singing and promoting her hugely successful song Dance the Night, the lead single from the soundtrack of the incredibly successful 2023 movie Barbie – in which Dua also had a cameo role as a mermaid Barbie.

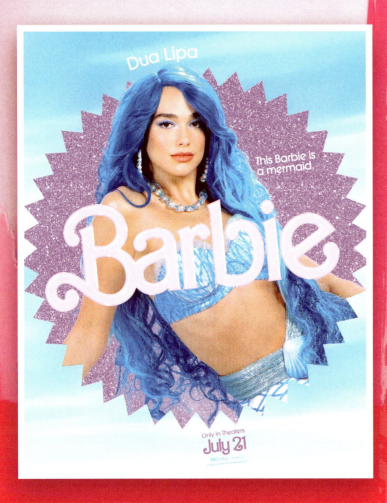

Dua at the UK premiere of Barbie at Cineworld Leicester Square, London, 2023.

Dua Lipa MWAH

She had also nabbed her first feature film role in spy thriller Argylle, directed and produced by Matthew Vaughn, released in February 2023. Dua was part of an all-star cast, including Samuel L. Jackson, Henry Cavill, Bryan Cranston, and Bryce Dallas Howard.

As well as all this, Dua had been in demand to promote the various luxury brands for which she is an ambassador. At the same time she was continuing with her popular podcast, her Service95 newsletter and its associated book club. She really was putting in the hours.

But when the album hit the airwaves, it proved worth the wait. Radical Optimism was critically acclaimed and gave Dua her first #1 debut in the UK and her second #1 album overall. She also clocked up the best opening week for a British female artist since Adele released 30 back in November 2021. In America the album reached #2 on the Billboard 200 chart, beating the #3 achieved by Future Nostalgia.

Dua said that British music from the 1990s had inspired her on this album, crediting Britpop and the style of trip-hop acts such as Portishead and Massive Attack in particular. It's been described as a step beyond the disco sound she promoted so successfully on Future Nostalgia, moving towards more of a 'neo-psychedelia' 1970s-style soundscape. In an interview with Rolling Stone magazine, Dua described the album as 'a psychedelic-pop-infused tribute to UK rave culture'.

Admiring critics all noted how Dua's voice had matured, becoming stronger and more commanding than ever with an alto range covering everything from mellow lows to girlish highs as she explores various styles, including dance-pop, ABBA-esque melodies, and more... she even performs an open-throated semi-yodel on Falling Forever.

ABOVE LEFT: Robert del Naja and Grant Marshall of Massive Attack.
ABOVE RIGHT: Beth Gibbons from Portishead.

Radical optimism for Dua's continued success...

RADICAL OPTIMISM

RELEASE DATE: May 2024   **RECORD LABEL:** Warner Bros. Music

TRACK LIST:

End of an era	Watcha Doing	Anything For Love
Houdini	French Exit	Maria
Training Season	Illusion	Happy for you
These Walls	Falling Forever	

What the critics said.....

Daily Mail (UK)
'Radical Optimism is a buoyant collection of breezy dance and luxuriantly produced pop that may well end up soundtracking the summer.'

Variety (US)
'Singles like Training Season and Illusion bolster the ephemeral, feel-good nature of 'Optimism.''

Daily Telegraph (UK)
'Dua Lipa miraculously maintains the air of someone who never puts a hair or dance step out of place, which we all know is much harder work than it looks.'

New York Times (US)
'The tracks on Radical Optimism are lavishly maximalist. They mingle sleek programmed sounds and luxurious live ones; bass, percussion and acoustic guitars bring a human touch, even as they're surrounded by sci-fi synthesizers and metronomic beats. It's an album of nonstop ear candy.'

A scene from Argylle, a film by Matthew Vaughn, 2023.

Radical optimism for Dua's continued success...

Dua Lipa MWAH

The intriguing title 'Radical Optimism' came when a friend used the term and Dua was struck by the ideas it gave her about going through chaos gracefully and feeling like 'you can weather any storm'. Although the tracks are about relationships and emotions, Dua doesn't bare her soul in the way that someone like Taylor Swift does, preferring to retain her mystique and making her lyrics more general, rather than revelatory.

She brought in some new collaborators for this album, including Australian musician Kevin Parker (of Tame Impala) and British producer Danny L. Harle. Dua has said that she had long wanted to work with Parker – even manifesting the event – as his 2015 album Currents is one of her favourites 'ever, ever' and 'completely changed my life'.

Parker and Harle's influence is heard throughout the album, from the upbeat End Of An Era, which sets the tone for the rest of the tracks right through to the closing number, the anthemic Happy For You, with hit singles, dance-pop bangers and catchy hooks in between.

The album's cover shot shows Dua floating in an ocean, seemingly calm despite the looming presence of circling sharks close by, further reflecting the album's theme of gracefully navigating chaos.

Radical optimism for Dua's continued success...

To promote her new music, Dua hit the road on a European tour including a string of dates during summer 2024 including headlining at Rock Werchter in Belgium, the Open'er Festival in Poland, and the Mad Cool Festival in Madrid.

In her UK homeland she topped the bill at the Glastonbury Festival on 28 June, then ends the year with a special show at London's Royal Albert Hall on 17 October 2024.

Dua live at Glastonbury Festival on the Pyramid Stage, June 2024.

Latest singles

DANCE THE NIGHT (MAY 2023)
This smash hit song from the blockbuster Barbie movie was #1 in the UK and Top 10 around the world including the US, Canada, Australia, and Europe. It was nominated for best song at the 2024 Grammy Awards.

HOUDINI (NOVEMBER 2023)
Houdini was the lead single from Radical Optimism, topping the charts around Europe and making #2 in the UK. It also topped the Billboard Dance/Electronic chart for 17 weeks.

TRAINING SEASON (FEBRUARY 2024)
The second single from Radical Optimism was Training Season which Dua sang live at the 2024 Grammy Awards. With its thumping bass, vocal harmonies and some interesting guitar rhythms, the song was another hit, making #4 in the UK charts.

ILLUSION (APRIL 2024)
The dance track Illusion was the third single from Radical Optimism, released on 11 April 2024. Combining French house influences with the album's psychedelic vibe, Dua has said it's one of her favourites from the album. It debuted at #9 in the British charts - the third consecutive Top Ten hit from the album.

Dua Lipa MWAH

Discography

35 SINGLES

singles

New Love – 21 August 2015*

Be the One – 30 October 2015 *

2016
Last Dance*

Hotter Than Hell *

Blow Your Mind (Mwah)*

2017
Scared to Be Lonely
  (with Martin Garrix)

Lost in Your Light (ft Miguel)*

New Rules *

Genesis

2018
IFGAF*

One Kiss (with Calvin Harris)

Electricity
  (with Silk City featuring Diplo
  and Mark Ronson)

Swan Song

Don't Start Now**

2020
Physical**

Break My Heart**

Hallucinate**

Un Día
  (One Day) (with J Balvin, Bad
  Bunny and Tainy)

Levitating (Solo or Ft DaBaby) **

Levitating
  (The Blessed Madonna remix)
  (ft Madonna and Missy Elliott)
  ***

Fever (with Angèle)

Real Groove Studio 2054 Remix
  (with Kylie Minogue)

2021
We're Good

Love Again

Cold Heart
  (Pnau remix) (with Elton John)

2022
Sweetest Pie
  (with Megan Thee Stallion)

Potion (ft Dua Lipa)

2023
Dance the Night

Houdini****

Discography

2024
Training Season****

Illusion****

Singles as a featured artist

2016
No Lie (Sean Paul ft Dua Lipa)

2018
If Only (Andrea Bocelli ft Dua Lipa)

2020
Sugar Remix (Brockhampton ft Dua Lipa)

Prisoner (Miley Cyrus ft Dua Lipa)

2021
Demeanor (Pop Smoke ft Dua Lipa)

Potion - **NEW UPDATE - POTION IS ACTUALLY A SINGLE FEATURING DUA LIPA** (with Calvin Harris, from his album Funk Wav Bounces Vol 2, and Young Thug)

album
Studio albums

Dua Lipa (June 2017)

Future Nostalgia (March 2020)

Radical Optimism (May 2024)

reissues
Dua Lipa: Complete Edition (October 2018)

Future Nostalgia: The Moonlight Edition (February 2021)

remixes
Club Future Nostalgia (with The Blessed Madonna - August 2020)

EPs
Spotify Sessions (July 2016)

Be the one (August 2016)

The Only (April 2017)

Live Acoustic (December 2017)

Deezer Sessions (April 2019)

* **from Dua Lipa**
** **from Future Nostalgia**
*** **from Club Future Nostalgia**
**** **from Radical Optimism**

Go Dua!

The music industry has a new feminist force for good. Dua's shiny brand of dance pop gems straddle R&B, synth-pop, hip hop, electro-funk, tropical house, and psychedelia – all with searing lyrics sung in her deep and emotive voice.

In April 2024 she was named by Time magazine as one of the most influential people of the year. The tribute to her was written by the singer-songwriter Patti Smith who said ...

'She moves with a lightness in a heavy world—bold, playful, and self-aware. She is thoughtfully outspoken for the oppressed and displaced. She founded an influential editorial platform, Service95, to cover cultural topics and address humanitarian concerns. She believes in family, is grateful to her parents and supportive of her siblings. She is driven, independent, and possesses a desire for knowledge. She appeals to future artists to be mindful of the world around them. She is herself, striving to redefine the pop-genre cosmos.'

High praise indeed from a performer who herself played a pioneering role in the American punk rock movement of the 1970s. But well deserved as pop megastar Dua looks set to continue making waves of her own. With almost 90 million followers and counting on Instagram, she is well placed to achieve everything she wished for as a young girl – even perhaps a media empire. Her Service95 venture already provides features on news topics and her recent interview with Apple CEO Tim Cook made headlines of its own.

She's smart and real – and of course, she really really wants everyone to dance!

Go Dua!